Langford Lovell Price

Money and it's Relations to Prices

Langford Lovell Price

Money and it's Relations to Prices

ISBN/EAN: 9783744731799

Printed in Europe, USA, Canada, Australia, Japan

Cover: Foto ©Suzi / pixelio.de

More available books at **www.hansebooks.com**

MONEY
AND ITS RELATIONS TO PRICES

*BEING AN INQUIRY INTO THE CAUSES,
MEASUREMENT, AND EFFECTS OF CHANGES IN
GENERAL PRICES*

BY

L. L. PRICE
Fellow of Oriel College, Oxford

LONDON
SWAN SONNENSCHEIN & CO. LIMITED
NEW YORK: CHARLES SCRIBNER'S SONS
1896

PREFACE

The material contained in this Book was collected for a course of lectures delivered by the author last summer as Newmarch Lecturer in Statistics at University College, London. The manuscript has since been re-written, some of the reasoning re-cast, and the figures revised.

The authorities, to whom reference has been made, are severally mentioned in the footnotes; and it only remains here to express a special debt of gratitude to two writers, to whom every student of the subject must feel that he owes peculiar acknowledgment. The name of Dr. Soetbeer is a household word in modern monetary statistics; and his fame is placed beyond dispute. The present author's obligations to him may be discovered in many passages. To Jevons' *Investigations in Currency and Finance* he is equally indebted; and a closer study of that book has confirmed his conviction that it may rank with the famous Report of the Bullion Committee among the classic productions of monetary science. If the earlier Report, in which the hand of Ricardo can be clearly traced, supplied the answer to the vexed problem of its day, it is no less indisputable that the intelligent study of the questions suggested by later movements of prices is impossible apart from an acquaintance with the *Investigations* of Jevons.

In dealing with matters, which have been, and are, the subject of embittered controversy, the author can hardly hope that his conclusions will command the approval or assent of all his readers. To claim freedom from bias would be an assumption, which would disprove itself by its very utterance; but he can honestly declare that he has avoided, rather than sought, debatable assertions, and that such opinions of this nature, as he may have expressed, are the result of an attempt to study the facts, and of reflection on the various, and sometimes opposite, explanations put forward by different inquirers.

L. L. P.

Oriel College, Oxford,
February, 1896.

CONTENTS

CHAP.		PAGE
I.	THE MEASUREMENT OF CHANGES IN PRICES	1
II.	THE ECONOMIC EFFECTS OF CHANGES IN PRICES	37
III.	THE RISE OF PRICES CONSEQUENT ON THE DISCOVERY OF AMERICA	70
IV.	THE FALL OF PRICES DURING THE EARLIER PART OF THE NINETEENTH CENTURY	104
V.	THE RISE OF PRICES CONSEQUENT ON THE DISCOVERIES OF GOLD IN CALIFORNIA AND AUSTRALIA	138
VI.	THE FALL OF PRICES DURING THE LAST TWENTY YEARS	170

MONEY
AND
ITS RELATIONS TO PRICES

CHAPTER I.

THE MEASUREMENT OF CHANGES IN PRICES.

SCIENTIFIC circles have been recently agitated over the discovery of a new element in the atmosphere; and the votaries of those moral and political studies, among which Economics claims a place, must have watched with interest, not unmingled with envy, the process by which the existence of that new element has been established. For the story of this latest addition to our scientific knowledge reads somewhat in this strain. In the course of researches in his laboratory the attention of the distinguished physicist,[1] with whose name the discovery is associated, was attracted to the presence of some disturbing influence, to which a place could not be assigned in the recognised scientific order. When suspicion had been thus aroused, a series of experiments was instituted, with the co-operation of another eminent scientist;[2] and those experiments were conducted, on the hypo-

[1] Lord Rayleigh.   [2] Professor Ramsay.

thesis of the possibility of an element hitherto unrecognised, with a view to demonstrating its existence and ascertaining its character and properties. The aim of these several experiments may be generally described as an attempt to isolate the phenomenon; and so successful did they prove that opposition was withdrawn and even distrust was apparently removed. The layman may presumably take the opinions expressed at a meeting of the Royal Society in January, 1895, as a verdict given by a jury of scientific experts in favour of the admission of Argon to a distinct place among the constituents of the atmosphere.[1]

The economist can hardly listen to such a story with feelings other than those of jealous admiration; for he can scarcely hope to discover its analogue in his own department of study. He may, indeed, like the student of natural science, form hypotheses; and he cannot expect to progress very far without their aid. But, when he wishes to bring them to the test of verification, he is practically debarred from the use of that powerful instrument for establishing scientific truth, which the physicist and chemist are able to employ with such admirable results. He can, indeed, observe phenomena, but he can rarely hope to experiment on them. Or, if some happy chance should permit an experiment, it will seldom allow of its being conducted in such a manner as to isolate the phenomena. The reason is simple and obvious. The subjects of his inquiry are not "inert" elements, but active men and women. They will not remain unmoved while

[1] *Cf. Edinburgh Review* for October, 1895, for a succinct account of the discovery. (No. 374.)

he observes them; and they will most assuredly resent being subjected to a deliberate experiment. Even the biologist encounters obstacles when he wishes to experiment on animal life; and the statesman, who should introduce a measure, or initiate a policy, not with a view to public utility, but with the single aim of establishing or disproving a scientific hypothesis by means of a carefully conducted experiment, would soon be driven—and not unnaturally—from office, if not from public life. Even if his avowed object were the promotion of general utility, and yet the experiment involved the possibility of a real injury to some one or other portion of the community, it is exceedingly doubtful whether he would be permitted to engage in it, or, once engaged, to carry it through. At any rate, it is certain that he would be debarred from conducting it under scientific conditions. The subjects of his inquiry would not remain passive. He would be unable to vary the conditions as the exigencies of the experiment required. He would not possess, or be allowed to exercise freely, the power of isolating some particular cause and observing it produce its effects undisturbed. His methods of inquiry must be subject to such defects as attach to the possibility of a plurality of causes. He is generally, if not always, reduced to a balancing of probabilities.

It is impossible to read any considerable portion of the abundant literature on money and kindred topics without being sensible of these difficulties; and they will confront us throughout the course of the inquiry on which we are entering. If, however, we recognise their existence from the outset, we shall obtain a more useful conception of the kind of evidence we can alone hope to secure, and of the character of the conclusions we must be content to establish.

Yet, if discouraging reflections like these are suggested by a contrast between the moral and political and the physical sciences, there is another characteristic of the present situation from which—paradoxical as the inference may appear—we may derive encouragement. It is no exaggeration to say that, if, on some rare occasions, the economist is permitted to witness, though not to initiate or conduct, an experiment, those occasions generally afford the material for a study in what, borrowing a term from physical science, we may perhaps call morbid pathology. To take examples from the subject before us, some such instance is presented as that of an opulent country, like the United States of America, finding itself, in consequence of monetary legislation, about which an opinion need not be expressed, in the throes of financial difficulties where its opulence is of no immediate avail. Or—to pass from the Western to the Eastern world—an experiment, viewed with favour by neither of the two parties engaged in internecine controversy on monetary matters, was lately instituted by the Indian Government, when it suspended the free coinage of silver; and economic students have been able to watch the course and observe the results of that experiment. They can see whether theories are verified or predictions unfulfilled. In both these instances—and parallels might be supplied from the same as from other departments of economic study—experiments are undoubtedly furnished for the instruction of the student, though even in these cases it is not easy, or indeed possible, to avoid the disturbing influences of a plurality of causes and an intermixture of effects. But the experiments are such that all, who concern themselves with the welfare of the community, would be glad, if they were able, to dispense with them, whatever their scientific value or interest. Experiments, it is true, of a more beneficent character are sometimes supplied by man or by nature; but there can be little doubt of the important, if melancholy, circumstance, that a morbid condition of the body politic is more calculated to attract notice, and to invite experiments, than a sound and healthy state. The beneficent experiments are not unlikely to escape attention—and, unless there be a disturbance of ordinary routine, men are averse to try experiments at all—while desperate or calamitous expedients force themselves into obvious and unpleasant prominence. It is when the machinery does not work smoothly that the mechanic is compelled to see what is wrong.

No elaborate argument is needed to support the contention that at the present time the monetary machinery is not working smoothly; nor is it necessary to demonstrate formally the lively interest which has of late been aroused in questions of monetary theory and practice.[1] The controversy between monometallist and bimetallist has been conducted with great vehemence, if not with great ability: and, difficult as it may seem to reach and retain the truth amid the din of contending argument, it is not easy to believe that such eager search for evidence, and such

[1] Professor Foxwell ("Transactions of Political Economy Circle of National Liberal Club," vol. ii., p. 174) has called attention to the significant fact of the issue of 1768 publications on the monetary question between 1871 and 1891 (according to Dr. Soetbeer's Bibliography).

persistent and incredulous examination of it, can have failed to result in some enlargement and improvement of scientific knowledge. Attention must of necessity have been directed to points hitherto unnoticed, and the weak links of a chain of argument could hardly have escaped the detection of such a searching scrutiny. Where a motive of so powerful a nature is supplied for research, it rarely fails to elicit new information, and there is scarcely a single point in received monetary theory which has not been called in question at some time or other during the controversy. Both on the purely statistical and on the more generally economic problems connected with money the debate has left its mark.

It is with the former class of problems that we shall be mainly occupied in the present inquiry, though it is impossible to disengage them entirely from general monetary theory. We may notice at the outset that Sir Robert Giffen, who is as competent as anyone to express an opinion, drew special attention, when examined before the Gold and Silver Commission,[1] to the "great improvement" which had been recently effected in monetary statistics. No doubt, as Professor Marshall urged before the same Commission,[2] there are important points on which we have as yet no statistical information of a reliable or adequate character, and there are some on which it is improbable that we can ever hope to obtain it. But, deficient as some of the statistical evidence unfortunately is, and doubtful as are some of the theoretical issues involved, certain broad conclusions emerge, and, even when obscured by the assertions and denials of

[1] *Cf.* Report, qq. 465, etc.   [2] *Ibid.*, q. 9629.

controversy, appear to have met with virtual admission, if not with open acknowledgment.

We propose to review the evidence on which those broad conclusions rest; and the special subject, to which we are going to address ourselves, may be summarily described as that of the causes and effects of changes in general prices; or, in other words, in the purchasing-power of money. In the first place [1] we shall inquire into the means that we possess for ascertaining and measuring such changes. We shall then proceed to review [2] their chief economic effects; and we shall conclude by a separate investigation into the prominent incidents of certain periods in English history when changes of a noteworthy nature occurred. The increase of the precious metals, which followed the discovery of America,[3] and that which in this century was connected with the new mines of California and Australia,[4] mark two periods when it is admitted that prices rose, and it is also allowed that the most obvious cause was the augmented production of the precious metals. With these periods we may contrast the somewhat obscure period of the beginning of this century,[5] and the period,[6] on the true explanation of which controversy is now raging, that, namely, which has elapsed since 1873. It will at least be conceded that the main characteristic of both these periods has been a fall in prices, although the particular cause of the fall may be stubbornly disputed. It will also perhaps be allowed—though this point may scarcely be granted so readily—that, if monetary changes have been the cause of the fall, those changes

[1] In chapter i. [2] In chapter ii. [3] Chapter iii.
[4] Chapter v.   [5] Chapter iv.   [6] Chapter vi.

may be roughly distinguished from the influx of the precious metals, which marked the other two periods, as partly due to artificial influences. A reversion to specie payments, such as that accomplished in 1819, though it be a reversion to a more healthy condition, and, the longer it is postponed, the more painful it generally becomes, is yet so far artificial that, like the suspension of those payments, and the issue of inconvertible paper, it is the deliberate action of men. The fall in prices since 1873, so far as it has been due to the demonetisation of silver and the adoption of a gold standard, must also be attributed to the action of men; while discoveries of the precious metals seem by contrast to be not improperly regarded as natural and unconscious. At any rate the distinction, if not unimpeachable, will be convenient.

In the first place, then, we propose to consider the means in our possession for measuring changes in general prices or alterations in the purchasing-power of money. For an inquiry into these means confronts us on the threshold of any investigation into the causes and effects of the changes. As we must diagnose the disease before we can venture to prescribe a remedy, so, to make our diagnosis adequate, we must be able to note the presence or absence of symptoms. In connection with this point of the means available for ascertaining and measuring changes in the purchasing-power of money, it may be confidently affirmed that the remark, which we previously hazarded, on the tendency of controversy to result in the improvement and enlargement of knowledge, finds abundant confirmation. A comparison of the methods pursued in the earlier and the later periods, of which we shall treat, will show, not merely that we are now in possession of an instrument, the capabilities of which were hardly recognised by those who investigated the circumstances of the earlier periods, but that we are sensible of the particular respects in which it is likely to be deficient, that we are able to devise and apply remedies for some of those defects, and that we have satisfied ourselves that, in spite of defects, the instrument is adequate for the purpose in hand. It would, no doubt, be untrue to say that a later generation can claim the credit of discovering the instrument; but it may at least be affirmed that earlier investigators did not attain to any adequate recognition of its capabilities or apply it scientifically to the problem before them.

In economic text-books three functions are generally assigned to money. It is described[1] as (1) a medium of exchange, (2) a measure or common denominator of value, and (3) a standard of deferred payments. To these three functions a fourth is sometimes added—that of a store of value—with which we need not concern ourselves. With regard to the first of these functions it is admitted that the essential characteristic of good money is that it should be generally acceptable, and any article, which satisfies this criterion, may serve as a medium of exchange. By acting in this character, and being constantly given and taken in exchange for other articles, money fulfils its second function, and becomes a convenient measure or common denominator of value. But, in the progress of society, as bargains are entered into

[1] Cf. Jevons' "Money"; F. A. Walker's "Money."

for longer and yet longer periods, the third function acquires additional prominence, and we need a standard of deferred payments. We do not merely require a common measure of articles and services to subserve the exigencies of the immediate moment, but we want a measure, which will enable us to compare those articles and services at different and distant times, and will remain valid during the interval. To discharge this function the paramount quality needed is that of steadiness; and the precious metals have established their claim to be used as money, partly because they have satisfied the criterion of general acceptability, and partly also because they have met, not indeed completely, but more sufficiently than any other article equally acceptable, the demand for stability. They have done so in consequence of their durable nature, as the annual production from the mines has, in ordinary times, been but a fraction of the mass in existence, and, therefore, their value has proved, comparatively speaking, independent of changes in supply. But it is not wholly independent. The conditions of their production are mutable; and, consequently, great and continued changes in the volume of production cannot, unless counteracted by alterations in demand, fail to produce an effect on their value, and to prejudice that stability which constitutes the basis of their fitness for a standard of deferred payments.

This liability to variation in value over intervals of time has led economic writers, both old and modern, to seek for a more stable measure; and it is evident that such a measure will at once satisfy more fully the criterion of a just standard of deferred payments, and, in the degree in which it fulfils this function, will furnish a gauge for testing the imperfections of the monetary standard, or, in other words, for estimating the changes in the purchasing-power of money or the alterations in general prices.

Adam Smith thought that he had discovered such a measure in labour. "Labour alone," he observed,[1] "never varying in its own value, is alone the ultimate and real standard by which the value of all commodities can at all times and places be estimated and compared." What he meant precisely by "labour never varying in its own value" has been disputed, and is not easy to ascertain; and we need concern ourselves with it the less, because, admirable and perfect as he held this standard to be in theory, he considered that, from lack of statistical data, it was not applicable to the practical measurement of changes in prices. "The current prices of labour at distant times and places can," he remarked, "scarce ever be known with any degree of exactness. Those of corn, though they have in few places been regularly recorded, are in general better known and have been more frequently taken notice of by historians and other writers. We must generally, therefore, content ourselves with them, not as being always exactly in the same proportion as the current prices of labour, but as being the nearest approximation which can commonly be had to that proportion." Accordingly, in a notable chapter,[2] to which we shall have again to refer, Adam Smith measures the alterations in the

---

[1] "Wealth of Nations," bk. i., ch. v.
[2] Ibid., bk. i., ch. xi., pt. iii.

value of silver by the fluctuations in the price of corn. But, throughout the discussion, he is careful to remind his readers that labour is the true measure, and that corn is only accurate so far as it corresponds. " Equal quantities of corn will," he observes, " in every state of society, in every stage of improvement, more nearly represent, or be equivalent to, equal quantities of labour, than equal quantities of any other part of the rude produce of land. Corn, accordingly, it has already been observed, is, in all the different stages of wealth and improvement, a more accurate measure of value than any other commodity or set of commodities." In these remarks there is not a little that is open to dispute, or, at least, inapplicable to the circumstances of the present day; but it cannot be doubted that, over long periods of time, the comparison, which Adam Smith instituted between corn and silver, did afford some indication—and perhaps the best which was then available—of the changes in the value of money. It is, however, no injustice to add that the improved method substituted in modern times is superior.

It is curious that this method should have been employed in a crude form by a writer on whom Adam Smith himself relied as an authority for statistical data, although he expressly dissented from his conclusions regarding the value of silver. " Bishop Fleetwood and Mr. Duprè de St. Maur are," he observed, " the two authors who seem to have collected, with the greatest diligence and fidelity, the prices of things in ancient times. It is somewhat curious that, though their opinions are so very different, their facts, so far as they relate to the price of corn at least, should coincide so very exactly." Bishop Fleetwood, in 1707, in his anonymous "Chronicon Preciosum,"[1] had sought to ascertain the changes in the value of money by comparing the prices at different periods, not of one commodity alone, but of a larger number,[2] including the wages of labour. His method was, no doubt, rough, and his statistical material deficient; but the conception, which underlay his calculations, was identical in principle with that which has since been elaborated in the so-called "index number."

Various other anticipations of this modern method have been discovered by the historical researches of Jevons and other writers. In the case of Lowe, writ-

---

[1] The full later title of the book was "Chronicon Preciosum; or, an Account of English Gold and Silver Money; the Price of Corn and other Commodities, and of Stipends, Salaries, Wages, Jointures, Portions, Day-labour, etc., in England for Six Hundred Years last past, showing from the Decrease of the Value of Money, and from the Increase of the Value of Corn and other Commodities, etc., that a Fellow, who has an Estate in Land of Inheritance, or a perpetual Pension of Five Pounds per Annum, may conscientiously keep his Fellowship, and ought not to be compelled to leave the same, tho' the Statutes of his College (founded between the years 1440 and 1460) did then vacate his Fellowship on such Condition." The name of the author was given in the later edition.

[2] Summarily enumerated as "corn, meat, drink, or cloth." The method is thus described: "You must neither take a very dear year to your prejudice, nor a very cheap one, in your own favour; nor indeed any single year, to be your rate; but you must take the price of every particular commodity, for as many years as you can (20, if you have them) and put them all together, and then find out the common price; and afterwards take the same course with the price of things for these last 20 years, and see what proportion they will bear to one another; for the proportion is to be your rule and guide." (*Cf.* chap. vi.) The inquiry into "stipends," etc., is made independently.

ing in 1822,[1] and Scrope,[2] some eleven years later, the primary object in view seems to have been that of securing justice in the matter of deferred payments and ensuring stability in money contracts; and Scrope gave to the pamphlet, in which he first advocated the method, the sub-title of "An Inquiry into the Nature of a Just Standard of Value." Sir George Evelyn, in a paper on "Some Endeavours to ascertain a Standard of Weight and Measure," in the "Philosophical Transactions" for 1798, propounded at the end of his paper a similar plan, and supplied a "general table" showing the changes in prices "from the Conquest," and, as became the connection in which the proposal appeared, the scientific object of measuring the changes in the value of money was exclusively predominant. Indeed, he apologised for appearing to "descend below the dignity of philosophy in such economical researches"; and, by the irony of fate, he has been criticised by historians for his "slovenly" treatment of the subject. The exact language used by Scrope may be quoted as a good definition of the nature and end of an index number. "It is proposed," he writes, "to correct the legal standard of value (or at least to afford to individuals the means of ascertaining its errors) by the periodical publication of an authentic price current, containing a list of a large number of articles in general use, arranged in quantities corresponding to their relative consumption, so as to give the rise or fall, from time to time, of the mean of prices, which will indicate, with all the exactness

[1] In his "Present State of England in regard to Agriculture, Trade, and Finance," pp. 276, etc., and Appendix to chapter ix.
[2] "Principles of Political Economy," p. 406.

desirable for commercial purposes, the variations in the value of money; and enable individuals, if they shall think fit, to regulate their pecuniary engagements by reference to this tabular standard."[1]

A similar method, with a similar object, was suggested in Porter's "Progress of the Nation";[2] but not until the occurrence of the Californian and Australian discoveries had resulted in an output of gold so immense as to be calculated to produce noteworthy changes in prices was the method of an index number applied in a systematic manner by Jevons to establish the fact of "A Serious Fall in the Value of Gold."[3] In his hands this instrument for measuring changes in general prices enjoyed the considerable advantage to be derived from the graphic method of statistics. But, great as was the advance in his treatment over the crude anticipations of earlier writers, it was reserved for another period, when changes in prices should again become a burning question—although it was the fall, and not the rise, to which attention was now directed—for a comparison to be made between several forms of index numbers and a critical examination to be instituted into their defects and capabilities. The exhaustive Reports[4] of a recent Committee of the British Association on the "best methods of ascertaining and measuring variations in the value of the Monetary Standard," together with the elaborate memoranda of Professor Edgeworth appended to

---

[1] *Cf.* "Principles of Political Economy," by G. Poulett Scrope, M.P., F.R.S., etc., pp. 406-407.
[2] Vol. ii., pp. 235, 236 (edition of 1838), sec. iii., ch. xii.
[3] *Cf.* "Investigations in Currency and Finance," ii., pp. 15, etc.
[4] *Cf.* Reports for 1887, 1888, 1889, and 1890.

those Reports, have enabled the student to advance a stage beyond that attained by Jevons in the theory, if not in the practice, of the index number; and the subject has also received instructive attention in other countries.[1]

Of these index numbers different varieties exist. Perhaps the simplest, though least scientific, is that of the *Economist*, and the method pursued by this newspaper may be briefly described. Twenty-two articles of a representative character have been selected for a comparison of the changes in their prices. A period has been chosen from which the comparison begins; and, in the special instance of the *Economist*, the average prices of the years 1845-50 have been taken as the starting-point. The prices of each article on the 1st of January and the 1st of July are noted, and a mean struck, and the prices at the starting-point are regarded in each case as equivalent to 100. In every subsequent year the percentage of the rise or fall of each article is added to, or taken away from, the original 100, and the separate figures are then added together to form a grand total, and, according as that total exceeds or falls short of the original grand total of 2200 reached in the quinquennial period from which the calculation starts, so is the change in the purchasing-power of money shown, whether by way of diminution or increase. Such is the character of the mere numerical calculation; but it is a common practice to supplement and illustrate the tables of figures by a curve of prices, which rises or falls in relation to a base line as the purchasing-power of

[1] *Cf.* Professor Edgeworth's article in *Economic Journal* for March, 1894, on "Recent Writings on Index Numbers."

money declines or advances. The aid of the graphic method of statistics may thus be invoked to bring within the range of easy comprehension the meaning of the numerical record; and no one, who has thus employed it, can have failed to appreciate its value.

Such is the nature of an index number as illustrated by perhaps the least scientific example. We may now proceed to inquire into the main respects in which it may possibly prove a defective measurement of changes in prices. In the first place the original data may be inadequate or even erroneous; and the earliest possibility of error lies in the ascertainment of the prices of the separate commodities. The first question to be asked concerns the trustworthiness of the records of prices on which the calculation is based. The difficulty, if not impossibility, of obtaining reliable data on the prices of labour led Adam Smith to content himself with the substitute of the prices of corn; and for a similar reason the compilers of index numbers have perforce to be satisfied with wholesale prices. This necessity is due to a lack of statistical data, but is not without compensation. It is true that retail transactions are more numerous, and in that sense more representative of the actions of the mass of the community. But, if comparisons are to be safely instituted, we must be able to reckon with some assurance on the probability that no great change is introduced in the articles forming the basis of the comparison. It is almost inevitable that, over considerable periods of time, the wholesale articles, of which the prices are recorded in an accessible and trustworthy form, will differ to some extent in quality, and so far the comparison will be vitiated, for the articles will in reality not be identical. But, in the case of retail as compared with wholesale prices, such differences of quality are largely multiplied.

The same lack of statistical data renders it necessary that the commodities, on the prices of which the calculation is based, should consist of raw materials, or at least of partly rather than of wholly manufactured goods; and it is probable that the general course of progress tends to diminish the cost of manufacture in comparison with the cost of obtaining the raw material. On the hypothesis of such a tendency we should expect that in times of rising prices an index number based to a preponderating or exclusive extent on raw materials, or on partly manufactured goods, would exaggerate the rise, and, in times of falling prices, would fail to indicate the full extent of the fall. But here again the limitations imposed by the statistical data available present insurmountable obstacles. The ideal index number might embrace, not a single article only, as that used by Adam Smith, nor a few, like those comprehended in the rough anticipations of earlier writers, such as Bishop Fleetwood, nor even the larger number of the later authorities, but all articles whatever bought and sold in a country. But this is an ideal far beyond the possibilities of realisation. Here, as elsewhere, we must perforce content ourselves with an approximation. Within the limitations of the statistical data we must make our list of commodities as representative as may be possible; and we must trust to the hypothesis, which careful investigation has shown to be reasonable, that, although our results are admittedly partial, they may be safely treated as typical. For it is a rational hypothesis that, while friction may delay the process, retail prices are likely in the end to follow the direction of wholesale, and it is even more probable that the prices of manufactured goods sold wholesale should conform with greater rapidity to changes in those of the raw materials of which they are made.

For the purely statistical purpose of ascertaining the changes in the purchasing-power of money, without framing any hypothesis on the cause of those changes, it is important that the material for the calculation should be as representative as is consistent with the paramount need of reliability; and, if it be sought to show that the change is due to some general cause, such as the increase or decline of the output from the mines, or of the available stock of the precious metals, such abundance is even more important, for it is by comprehensiveness alone that we can hope to eliminate the influence of special causes affecting particular commodities. The more numerous the commodities, the more likely it is that some special cause affecting some one commodity in some particular manner will be counteracted by some other cause affecting another commodity in an opposite manner. But to attain this end the commodities should be independent of one another,[1] and manufactured goods can scarcely be said to be independent of the raw material of which they are made, or goods sold retail of those same goods exchanged in the wholesale market. Given, therefore, sufficient variety

---

[1] *Cf.* Professor Edgeworth's Memorandum in British Association Report for 1887. It is a principle of statistical inquiry that sample statistics may be as effective as complete statistics, and the difficulty turns on the determination of the question whether in the particular investigation the samples are truly representative.

of commodities, it is not a defect from this point of view that the prices should be wholesale, and, in the main, those of raw materials.

The hypothesis that the change is due to some expansion or contraction in the supplies of money has an important bearing on the next particular regarding the construction of an index number, to which our attention will be directed. This concerns the starting-point of the calculation. A consideration of the circumstances, to which allusion was made when the suitability of the precious metals as a standard of deferred payments was under discussion, leads to the conclusion that any change in the purchasing-power of money, which is due to an increased or diminished supply from the mines, is likely to be evident only over considerable intervals of time. The annual production is so small in comparison with the stock in existence that its ordinary influence from year to year is unimportant and unnoticeable. But, if some considerable change continues to operate for a period of years, its effects will be manifest in an alteration in purchasing-power.

On this ground Adam Smith was justified in measuring the fluctuating value of silver by the price of corn. He was aware that that price might vary greatly from one year to another in consequence of the character of the seasons; but he held that, over a considerable interval of time, the real value of corn did not materially alter, as the improvement in the efficiency of human labour counterbalanced the increasing price of cattle, the chief agricultural instrument. His explanation may be inadequate or even erroneous, but his conclusion was broadly true; and he expressly allowed in part of his calculations for the disturbing effects of a series of bad seasons.

It is curious to note that investigations into the prices of a hundred years later led Tooke,[1] taking short periods of year by year, to attribute everything, or almost everything, to the influence of the seasons. To him, perhaps, is largely owing the publicity of Gregory King's classical table exhibiting the enormous and disproportionate effect produced by a scarcity of corn on the price of that article. But there can be little doubt that he failed to detect the influence of a broad cause because he concentrated attention on the special circumstances of successive single seasons or short periods of years, and on the conditions affecting mainly one article alone. The criticism passed by Jevons[2] on predecessors like Tooke, that they seemed to lack the power of extracting from their tables of prices the information, which was really contained, is not undeserved.

One of the most important services, indeed, of that graphic method of statistics, of which Jevons himself made such felicitous use, has consisted in the detection of the broader movements of prices and their separation from minor and more passing disturbances. From Jevons' "Letters"[3] we learn that he believed that he had a "capacity of seeing the sameness and difference of things"; and his "Investigations in Currency and Finance" furnish abundant proof of the possession and use of this faculty. Yet it may be questioned whether, without the aid of the graphic

---

[1] *Cf.* his "History of Prices."
[2] *Cf.* "Investigations in Currency and Finance," p. 120.
[3] *Cf.* "Letters and Journal of W. Stanley Jevons," p. 176.

method, with its curves of prices, it would be possible to discern clearly in any mere tables the "sameness and difference of things." No one, at least, who has studied with care such a curve of general prices, extending over a sufficient period, can have failed to observe the differing character of the fluctuations. The periods of alternating prosperity and depression, which have been established by statistical research, aided by economic reasoning, as the normal characteristic of modern commerce and industry, and appear to occupy about decennial intervals, can be distinguished by the eye at once from the minor temporary fluctuations, due to some accident of supply or demand, which yet leave their mark on the general curve, and from what Cournot called [1] the "secular movement" up and down, indicating the fall and rise in the purchasing-power of money. Such a curve may be said to furnish that ocular demonstration which is, perhaps, more convincing than any argumentative process; and for the scientific construction of these curves the student has waited till comparatively recent times.

In order, therefore, to arrive at the broad changes in the purchasing-power of money, which extend over considerable intervals of time, and to detect the influence of a common general cause affecting in a similar manner the prices of a number of separate commodities, it is necessary to eliminate, not merely the minor temporary fluctuations, which may be traced to some passing accident in the supply or the demand of particular commodities, but the recurring movements of alternating expansion and contraction

[1] "Principes de la Théorie des Richesses," p. 149.

of credit. For this reason it is held to be more appropriate that the starting-point of the calculation in an index number should be the prices, not of a single year, but of an average of years. They should not be unduly exalted or depressed by transitory circumstances of the market or by credit fluctuations. They should represent the average level of commercial activity, and not the fever of speculative excitement or the torpor of stagnation. If the purchasing-power of money is falling, prices should tend to be higher during every point of the succeeding credit cycle than they were at the corresponding points of the preceding. They should be higher when the wave of speculation is at its crest; they should be higher also in the trough of depression. If, on the other hand, the purchasing-power of money is rising, prices should be lower both during the flow and during the ebb of credit. They should fall with that ebb, but they should fall still lower in consequence of the "secular change" in the value of money. To render valid such comparisons it is desirable to select as the starting-point of the calculation a set of prices, which may be regarded as independent of the special influence of expanding or contracting credit, and should accordingly be based on an average of years, which will include or neutralise the effects alike of excessive speculation and extreme depression.

A third consideration with regard to an index number, which deserves some notice, is also connected with the starting-point of the calculation. The *Economist* number adopts, as we have observed, a mean between the prices of the articles included in its comparison taken on the 1st of January and the

1st of July of every year. But the practice of another index number—that of Mr. Sauerbeck—might be substituted, and a yearly average obtained from the prices of each month. Or we might content ourselves with a single set of prices taken on some one date in each successive year, or we might pursue some more refined and elaborate method. The question, however, of the particular method adopted is not, it would seem, of very great importance. The point, to which it is essential to attend, is that the prices should be taken at the same time, and in the same way, in the subsequent years as in the year or years from which the calculation starts. It is an established doctrine of statistics that figures, which are themselves erroneous, may yet be safely employed for purposes of comparison, if it is possible to reckon with sufficient certainty on the uniform recurrence of the error. The importance of this consideration has been already observed when the greater liability of retail than wholesale commodities to changes in quality was noted; and, without neglect of the claims of accuracy, it may be held that, so long as the prices are ascertained in the same manner and at the same time in the successive years of the series, if they fail to be truly representative or perfectly exact at the outset, they will fall short to about the same extent throughout the calculation, and the error will therefore fail to vitiate the comparison. The aim in view is that of comparison, and for this purpose the error can be eliminated.

A point of greater subtlety, and not less difficulty, is raised by the consideration of the various methods of arriving at the general average from the particular prices. The method followed by the *Economist* is comparatively easy and simple; and it may be laid down as a broad principle that, the simpler and easier the calculation, the less danger will there be of chance mistakes. But to obtain a true measure of the changes in general prices other considerations must be taken into account. Economists of mathematical attainments have devoted no small attention to the most exact and appropriate method of reaching the general average; but for the purposes of the present inquiry it is perhaps unnecessary to enter on any abstruse or technical mathematical reasoning. It may be possible to put into ordinary intelligible language the main questions at issue.

Three chief modes of taking the average have been distinguished in discussions on the question. These are (1) the Arithmetical Mean, (2) the Geometrical Mean, and (3) the Median. The first of these is the method commonly adopted in ordinary life, and usually intended by the plain man when he speaks of striking an average. It consists simply in adding together the changes in the prices of the separate commodities and dividing the total by the number of commodities. The method, as Professor Edgeworth remarks in one of the memoranda[1] to which we have referred, is recommended by its very simplicity, and by its accordance with the general results of common experience. But its adequacy to the measurement of changes in general prices has been questioned, and, although the tendency of subsequent opinion has inclined in its favour, Jevons himself preferred the more elaborate process of the geometric mean.

[1] *Cf.* Report of British Association for 1887, pp. 283, etc.

This may be briefly described in his language. "To take the geometric mean of two ratios," he remarks,[1] "we must multiply them together and extract the square root of the product." He rests the superiority of this process over the arithmetic mean on the consideration that the easier method "exaggerates" "the prices which have risen at the expense of those which have fallen"; and Professor Edgeworth has shown [2] both on *a priori* and *a posteriori* grounds that some such defect may conceivably attach. In forming estimates, he remarks, there appears to be a tendency to err by excess more than by defect, and this tendency may influence the demand felt for an article on the ground of its utility. There may be more exaggerations than under-estimates of that utility. Moreover, he adds, it is obvious that, while "a price may rise to any amount," it "cannot sink below zero." Prices may therefore "be apt to deviate much more in excess than in defect." And, lastly, "tacit combinations" between dealers "may prevent prices from falling as low as from time to time they otherwise would, according to the law of supply and demand." These *a priori* considerations Professor Edgeworth supports by an examination of certain well-known prices; and, translating his reasoning into the language of curves, he shows that prices may conceivably tend to group themselves, not in the "symmetrical curve," which corresponds to the arithmetic mean, where the extremes range themselves similarly on either side of an intermediate position, but in the "unsymmetrical curve of which the range in excess is

---

[1] "Investigations in Currency and Finance," p. 24.
[2] *Cf.* Report as quoted above.

greater than in defect." To this unsymmetrical curve the geometric mean more nearly corresponds.

Professor Edgeworth himself, however, is inclined to favour the use of a third method—that of the median [1]—and he holds that theory and practice combine to show that, where the prices are numerous, the symmetrical curve of the arithmetic mean tends to be realised, while the employment by Jevons of the geometric mean, according to his own confession, was inadequate to prevent the undue influence on the general average of the special circumstances affecting the price of cotton during the American War, and he was compelled to seek and apply a further corrective.[2] The median, on the other hand, Professor Edgeworth argues, is adapted both to cases where the curve of prices is symmetrical and to those where it is not. It consists of that quantity which has as many observations above it as below it. It is manifestly easier to reach than the geometric mean, although, as Jevons showed, that method was simplified by the use of tables of logarithms; and it is not more difficult to handle than the arithmetic mean, while it makes greater allowance for the possibility of error.

Akin to this question of the appropriate method of striking the general average is the point whether all the commodities included in the calculation should be considered of the same importance. Do they all play the same part in the business of life? Do they

---

[1] *Cf.* Report, pp. 284, 288, 291, and also paper on "Some New Methods of Measuring Variation in General Prices," in *Statistical Journal* for June, 1888, vol. li., pt. ii.

[2] *Cf.* "Investigations," p. 39. Jevons repeated for the years 1861 and 1862 the low prices of 1860.

equally afford, by the changes in their prices, the means of measuring the alterations in the general purchasing-power of money? The assignment of different degrees of importance to different articles is technically known as "weighting," and may be effected in various ways. More than one place in the list of commodities embraced in the calculation may be allotted to the more important, or the less important may be removed altogether. Each commodity may be multiplied by a figure representing its comparative importance and based upon respective consumption. An attempt may even be made to allow a different weight on this account in different years of the series. A regard for theoretical accuracy undoubtedly suggests the employment of some such method of weighting, and it is explicitly adopted in the case of some well-known index numbers. For a full discussion of the general considerations, by which this weighting should be regulated, reference may be again made to Professor Edgeworth's Memoranda;[1] and here it may merely be noted as the outcome of his mathematical reasoning that an error in the weighting seems of far less importance than an error in the prices in its effect on the correctness of the result.[2]

Such are the chief points, which appear to deserve attention in the construction of an index number, and such are the main possibilities of error. In passing them in review we have aimed, not so much at demonstrating the adequacy or insufficiency of the method, as at proving that its conditions and limita-

[1] And to the paper quoted above in the *Statistical Journal* for June, 1888.
[2] *Cf.* Report of the British Association for 1888, p. 200.

tions have formed the subject of systematic inquiry, and that, if, as is undoubtedly true, it is allowed a recognised place by economists and statisticians, this position is not conceded from ignorance of its real characteristics, or of its possible defects. It is no exaggeration to say that the index number is now generally regarded, not merely as an useful, but as an indispensable, instrument in any scientific inquiry into changes in the purchasing-power of money.

The chief numbers formed and used in recent years may be briefly enumerated. That of the *Economist* has been already described. The prices, from which the calculation starts, are those of an average based on the prices of the quinquennium extending from 1845 to 1850. The commodities selected are 22 in number, and their prices in each successive year of the series are a mean of those obtained on the 1st of January and the 1st of July. The general average is a simple arithmetic mean.

In his investigations into the fall in the value of gold in the middle of the century Jevons employed [1] much the same prices as those of the *Economist* index number, which was, indeed, a continuation of his own, except that, by grouping, his 39 articles were reduced to 22. He took a mean between the highest and the lowest prices (indicating different qualities) of each article recorded in the middle of the month, from which he obtained the yearly average by a simple arithmetic mean, and by the same process he reached the average of the period 1845-50 from which his calculation started. But for his general average he adopted the geometric and not the arithmetic mean.

[1] *Cf.* "Investigations," chapter ii., sec. xiii.

He also calculated [1] the changes in the prices of 79 less important commodities—which were in most cases distinct from the original 39—by a method generally similar.

A variation of the *Economist* index number was employed by Mr. Palgrave in 1886 in a Memorandum prepared for the Depression of Trade Commission.[2] The same 22 articles were used, but the period 1865-69 was substituted as the starting-point of the calculation, and an endeavour was made to "weight" the measurement by assigning to each article a figure representing its "relative importance." This figure was obtained by calculating the value of the quantity of each article annually consumed in the United Kingdom in the twenty years 1865-85; and a similar calculation was applied by Mr. Palgrave to 22 French articles.

A slightly different method of weighting has been used by Sir Robert Giffen in the construction of index numbers based on the prices of imports and exports.[3] Taking a particular year (which he stated in evidence before the Gold and Silver Commission to be 1875, although he added that the process had been tested by comparison with the results obtained from the selection of some other year), he assigns a proportionate number to each article "according to the proportion of its value to the total value of the imports and exports respectively." "The percentage of rise or fall" is "multiplied" by "the proportionate number" thus assigned, and "divided by the sum of the

[1] "Investigations," ch. ii., sec. xvii.   [2] *Cf.* Third Report, p. 329.
[3] *Cf.* "Essays in Finance," first series, xiv.; second series, i.; and Report of Gold and Silver Commission, qq. 709, etc.

proportionate numbers." The full index number of 100 is not reached because in the case both of the imports and the exports the number of articles is limited for which it is possible to obtain prices by dividing the values by the quantities (the method by which the prices are ascertained). The aggregate index number, accordingly, for the imports is 81·16, and for the exports 65·8; and Sir Robert Giffen expressly retains these lesser numbers in order to show that all the imports and exports are not embraced in the calculation. The prices of single years—those of 1840 for the exports and of 1854 for the imports—are taken as the starting-point.

Two other index numbers have attracted general notice. Of these that of Mr. Sauerbeck is based on English prices.[1] Forty-five articles are comprised, and their representative character may be inferred from the fact that they embrace all the articles in the United Kingdom, of which statistics exist, and the value—whether they are produced in the country or imported from abroad—exceeds a million pounds. Taking monthly prices, Mr. Sauerbeck strikes a simple average for the year; and he starts with the average prices of the decade extending from 1867 to 1877, which, he states, are in the "aggregate" found to be equivalent to the average of the twenty-five years from 1853 to 1877. A simple arithmetic mean is adopted as the general average, but it is tested in two ways, which are thus described by Mr. Sauerbeck.

[1] *Cf.* paper on "Prices of Commodities during the last Seven Years" in *Statistical Journal* for June, 1893, vol. lvi., pt. ii., evidence given before Gold and Silver Commission, qq. 878, etc., and article in *Economic Journal* for June, 1895, vol. v., no. 18.

One is that of weighting each article according to its importance on the average of the three years 1889-91. The other is that of "calculating the quantities in the United Kingdom at their actual value" ("the production on the basis" of Mr. Sauerbeck's own price tables, "and the imports at the Board of Trade values") "and at the nominal values on the basis" of the average prices of the decade from which the calculation starts.

The other index number, to which reference should be made, is that of the late Dr. Soetbeer.[1] As many as 114 articles were included in his Tables, of which 100 were Hamburg prices, and 14 English. The average of the years 1847-50 was taken as the starting-point of the calculation. The articles were divided into eight large groups, and an index number obtained for each group in succession, and then a number was reached for the whole by regarding each of the subordinate groups as equally important, although they did not in each case contain the same number of commodities. This process amounted, as Sir Robert Giffen has observed,[2] to a kind of weighting.

Such are the best known varieties of index numbers used in recent years in England, although the list is not exhaustive. It will be noticed that they exhibit differences of detail in construction. All refer to wholesale prices; and those of the *Economist*, of Mr. Palgrave

[1] *Cf.* "Materialien zur Erläuterung und Beurteilung der Wirtschaftlichen Edelmetall-verhältnisse und der Währungsfrage," of which a translation is appended to the Final Report of the Gold and Silver Commission, and an American translation by Professor Taussig is appended to Reports from the Consuls of the United States on Bimetallism in Europe. (No. 87, December 1887.)

[2] *Cf.* Report of Gold and Silver Commission, q. 733.

and of Mr. Sauerbeck deal, speaking broadly, with
the same commodities. But in this respect those of
Sir Robert Giffen and of Dr. Soetbeer are different;
and the starting-points selected, and the methods of
assigning weight—where such methods are employed
—are not identical. Yet it is undoubtedly the case
that the broad results are similar, and that a marked
tendency in one direction is manifest. Nor is the
technical reasoning of Professor Edgeworth's Memoranda,[1] or the authoritative pronouncement of the
Gold and Silver Commissioners, and of the Committee
appointed by the British Association, at variance
with this conclusion. That errors tend to cancel
one another, and that there may be less error in a
conclusion than in the data from which it is
deduced, and that, if different methods do not differ
widely from one another, it is probable that they
do not differ widely from the ideal method, may
seem "hard sayings" to the plain man, but they are
the outcome of scientific inquiry, and they are not
easy to disprove. On the adequacy of the method to
determine nice points of detail doubt may indeed be
felt, but of its sufficiency as a measure of the broad
changes in the value of the monetary standard it may
be affirmed, without fear of serious contradiction, that
it has been scientifically tested, and that it has passed
the test. Indeed, although, as we have noticed, it
may seem desirable to weight the prices, which form
the basis of the calculation, when we view the matter
theoretically, a simple arithmetic mean has been found
in practice to yield results, which are not only, with

[1] *Cf.* especially that in the Report of the British Association for 1888.

rare exceptions, adequate, but are also generally similar to those obtained by the more elaborate processes.

If an index number is intended to be used as a tabular standard[1] for deferred payments, and to receive the sanction—permissive or compulsory—of the Legislature, it should undoubtedly be constructed with a close regard to scientific requirements. Nor is it possible to avoid entirely the danger of some variation in quality, which may vitiate *pro tanto* the comparison; and changes may be gradually and insensibly introduced in market-quotations of prices which, over an interval of years, amount to a real difference. No doubt, again, regarded from the standpoint of the ordinary consumer, retail prices are the more important consideration in his budget, and they may only conform with some delay to wholesale prices, which, from the point of view of the producer, are of paramount importance. But that within its limits the index number, as generally constructed, is an useful, if not indispensable, instrument of economic and statistical inquiry, and that, within its limits also, it is an instrument sufficient for its purpose, may be regarded as a fact established after close investigation.

In conclusion, a further question may now be raised, but must be answered more fully when we investigate the special circumstances of particular periods. The index number affords the means of solving a statistical problem. It registers and measures the changes in the purchasing-power of money. It indicates the alterations of general prices. But the further problem at once arises of determining the cause to which those

[1] *Cf.* below, p. 37.

changes are due; and here the answer of the index number must, from the conditions of the case, be by itself inconclusive. But it may be used to corroborate other evidence. Does the cause, it may be asked, lie with the commodities or with the money? There is undoubtedly a change in the relation between them, but to which is the alteration due? To this knotty question we shall have to return, and at the present stage of our inquiry we must be content with very general considerations. If by other evidence we can establish the probability that the cause lies mainly on the side of the money, we can then look for confirmation or the reverse to the index number. We must remember that the cause will in all probability produce its full results only after an interval of time, and that it will exercise its influence by gradual and partial stages. To the extent, no doubt, that it is operative its effects will in reality be uniform, but it will probably produce some counteraction, and therefore they will not seem to be uniform. We may at once pronounce in a sense true, and yet misleading, the common assertion that, if a change of prices be due to an expansion or contraction of the supplies of money, the rise or fall must be universal and immediate. To corroborate other evidence of the presence of such a cause, the index number need only indicate a general and a gradual change.

Again, the larger and more representative the basis of construction, the more likely it is that the change indicated by the index number in the relation between commodities and money is due, not to the commodities, each of which may be specially affected by some one cause, probably different from, or opposed to, that which is operating on some other commodity, but to the money given and taken in exchange. The particular influences are thus likely to be eliminated, and the result, as shown by the index number, to be due to some common cause. It is possible that this common cause may lie on the side of the commodities; but the index number tends to lessen the importance to be ascribed to a separate investigation into the circumstances of each individual commodity. It diminishes the confidence sometimes manifested that such an investigation alone furnishes an adequate explanation of changes in general prices, and that it is needless to look beyond for a common cause. These narrow observations are perhaps more often an obstacle than an aid to the attainment of correct perspective; for particular causes are not difficult to discover if we set ourselves to find them, but the search is often prejudicial to a general view. It must, however, be admitted that the difficulty of a plurality of causes and an intermixture of effects is one from which the economist is rarely, if ever, freed; and he is generally compelled to be content with a balancing of probabilities. Such appear to be the broad conclusions on the evidence furnished by index numbers of the causes of alterations in the purchasing-power of money.

CHAPTER II.

THE ECONOMIC EFFECTS OF CHANGES IN PRICES.

In the last chapter we were occupied with the statistical measurement of changes in general prices. We noted the characteristics and failings of index numbers, and the chief points of difference in their construction. They may be designed to fulfil two purposes—the one scientific, and the other practical. The scientific end is the measurement of changes in the value of money, and the practical object is the correction of its defects as a standard. To the consequences of those imperfections we shall now turn our attention.

That changes occur from time to time in the purchasing-power of money, that such an instrument as an index number may be usefully employed to register those changes, and that in certain cases its substitution for the more imperfect monetary standard may be desirable, are conclusions which are naturally suggested; and in this application to practical ends the index number has sometimes received the name of a "multiple legal tender" or a "tabular standard."[1] Objections may be raised to the employment of such a standard on the ground of unfamiliarity, or perhaps of a certain refinement of calculation, which is likely to confuse or alarm the plain man, and it may

[1] *Cf.* Jevons: "Money and the Mechanism of Exchange," ch. xxv.

easily prove to be cumbrous or even impossible. But it can hardly be doubted that its use might prevent injustice, because it would correct the imperfections of the monetary standard. Into the nature of those imperfections we may now inquire.

They arise in connection, not with the use of money as a medium of exchange, or as a common denominator or measure of value, in the senses distinguished in the text-books, but with its employment as a standard of deferred payments. It is important to lay stress on this point at the outset, because in some current discussions it seems to be neglected or forgotten. It is unnecessary that money in each of its uses should be identical in form or material. A good medium of exchange may not prove an excellent standard of deferred payments. The paramount quality demanded for the one is general acceptability, and the most important requisite needed for the other is stability. It is not impossible that commodities may be found possessing the one quality, which are yet deficient in the other, and we may reject them for the one use without dismissing them from the other. Innovators, anxious to improve the standard of deferred payments, may fairly claim that they are not answered by the assertion that the substitute, which they propose, would be an inconvenient medium of exchange, while reformers, intent on the introduction of a new coinage, or the reformation of the old, may conceivably neglect the requirements of a stable standard of deferred payments. The instructed economist would seek, if it be possible, to combine both advantages in a sound monetary system—that of a convenient medium of exchange and that of a stable standard of deferred payments—but he would be ready to recognise that to satisfy this dual criterion it is not necessary, it is even unlikely, that the medium and the standard should be identical.

It is then as a standard of deferred payments that imperfections have been discovered in the precious metals. From the consideration that the conditions of their production are mutable it is evident that such imperfections cannot be avoided; but, owing to the fact that in ordinary circumstances the annual output is small compared with the stock in existence, these imperfections cannot usually be detected until after an interval, and it requires a considerable and continued change to bring them into noticeable prominence. For the purposes, therefore, of a measure of value over short intervals, the precious metals are more suited than other commodities, and they are by comparison stable. But for a standard of deferred payments their fitness is less evident; for their stability no longer remains unimpeachable. In ordinary circumstances they may be more stable than any single commodity; but at times of considerable change in the volume of production they may be compelled to yield the prerogative, and in any event they are less stable than a standard expressly designed, like an index number, to register and counterbalance their imperfections. The example quoted by Adam Smith[1] of Colleges, a proportion of whose rents was by the wisdom and equity of the Elizabethan statesman fixed in corn and not in money, and thus secured from the loss consequent on the fall in the value of silver, which followed the discovery of America, has

[1] "Wealth of Nations," bk. i., ch. v.

become classical; and constructors of index numbers, from Lowe and Scrope onwards, have generally been no less concerned with the practical end of ensuring justice in monetary contracts than with the purely scientific object of discovering and measuring the alterations in the purchasing-power of money.

For in any but a primitive society the number and importance of deferred payments are at once considerable and progressive. If debtor is not to benefit at the expense of creditor, or creditor to inflict an injury on debtor, the purchasing-power of money should remain unaltered during the time that the loan is current. The monetary expression, in which the debt is contracted and repaid, should correspond with the real amount of commodities, which the money can command. Nor is it conducive to the security and advance of society that constant changes should be made in a number of payments, which are conveniently treated as fixed; and yet, if the purchasing-power of money alters, a strict regard for equity would dictate such a change. The fact is that the ordinary business of society proceeds on the assumption that the purchasing-power of money continues unchanged, and on such an assumption alone can permanence be given to social arrangements. So imbued indeed with the spirit of this assumption is the average man that it requires an effort of reasoning, and a disturbance of ingrained habit, to realise the unquestionable fact that the money of ordinary use is not thus perfectly stable. The liability noted by Adam Smith[1] in writers aware of the errors of the Mercantile System, to allow insensibly the "lands, houses, and consumable goods,"

---

[1] "Wealth of Nations," bk. iv., ch. i.

with which they started in their reasoning, to "slip out of their memory," and to continue the argument as if gold and silver were the only form of wealth, finds its analogy in the conception of the stability of money entertained in the mind of the plain man; and hence partly, no doubt, his aversion to the refinements of the tabular standard. But his reluctance or inability to form any clear or abiding recognition of the fact does not make the fact itself untrue or unimportant, and he is rudely awakened from his slumbers if some sudden change occurs.

On the injurious effects of such sudden change no dispute is raised. It is generally agreed that rapid and extreme fluctuations in the purchasing-power of money are purely mischievous, if they are not calamitous. The lesson taught by excessive issues of inconvertible paper is written deeply on the memory of nations of advanced civilisation. There are countries, it is true, where the lesson is not fully learnt, and there may be times among progressive nations when for the moment it is forgotten. Yet the skill and discretion shown[1] by the Bank of France during the war with Germany, when specie payments were suspended, and the paper currency became for the time inconvertible, may be justly regarded as constituting an advance upon the management of our own Bank of England in similar circumstances during the Napoleonic war, and that management is itself in marked contrast with many an epoch of calamitous disaster occasioned in other countries by excessive issues before and since. For the dislocation of contracts produced, and the fever of speculation en-

[1] *Cf.* Dunbar: "Theory and History of Banking," p. 125.

gendered, are acknowledged to be unmistakable evils; and so great is the mischief occasioned that, when the inevitable period of contraction ensues, it seems almost better, in spite of the severity of the suffering, that it should be effected with as little delay as possible, and that the necessary pain should not be mitigated by a gradually increasing application of the remedy. The disease has made such inroads that the knife or the cautery is kinder than bandage or ointment; and the significant feature of a period of excessive issues, thus rapidly terminated, is that the rise of prices advances with a speed, which allows of no interval for the readjustment of bargains, and the quick-witted rascal profits at the expense of the honest citizen.

It is then no more and no less than an economic truism that sudden and excessive fluctuations are unmitigated ills; and the only reason why rapid contraction of inconvertible paper may be preferable to a more gradual process is that the malady to be overcome has passed beyond the reach of mere alleviatory remedies. It may, no doubt, be described as a case of "kill or cure"; and the death-rate is high and the survivors are few. In itself the process of sudden contraction, like that of sudden expansion, is evil, but it is demanded by the conditions of the situation.

If, however, it be admitted on the one hand that sudden and excessive fluctuations are mischievous or calamitous, it must on the other be remembered that perfect stability is unattainable. The recurrence of alternating periods of activity and depression—of expanding and contracting credit—is an established fact in the modern economy of commerce; and the precious metals themselves are constantly undergoing change, whether in the direction of a rise or a fall of value. To look for complete stability is to listen to "counsels of perfection" rather than the lessons of universal experience. As we saw, the instinctive habit of regarding the standard as itself immutable, while changes take place in the objects, the value of which it is employed to measure, prevents the quick recognition of alterations in the general purchasing-power of money; and in ordinary cases those changes, unlike the issues of inconvertible paper, are actually so gradual as to seem insensible. Even, when new discoveries of the precious metals are made, and the annual output is largely increased, it has to exert its influence on the stock in existence, and to find its way into the channels of business, and this process is not accomplished in a day or a week or a year. Nor are the effects of contraction less gradually felt or imperceptibly manifested. An alteration in prices, due to an increase or diminution in the available supplies of the precious metals, when contrasted with the demands made upon them, is not, as common opinion often apparently believes, and sometimes noisily asserts, immediate or uniform or universal.

For the mode, in which the new supplies find their way into the business of the world, is thus conceived by economic writers.[1] In the countries of the mines themselves the result of an increased output is to lower the value of the precious metals by reason of

[1] *Cf.* Ricardo on "The High Price of Bullion;" J. S. Mill: "Principles of Political Economy," bk. iii., ch. xix.; F. A. Walker: "Money," ch. iii.

their relative abundance, and to increase the prices of the commodities for which they are given and taken in exchange. The monetary value of the commodities is therefore higher in the countries of the mines than it is elsewhere, and the value of the precious metals themselves is relatively lower. A tendency is accordingly set in motion to increase the imports into the countries of the mines in order to realise by their sale these higher prices, and to send the precious metals elsewhere to places where they will command a greater purchasing-power by reason of their relative scarcity. Together with the increase of imports into the countries of the mines, there will also be a tendency to a diminution of exports of commodities apart from the precious metals: for other countries will be disinclined to pay the increased prices which they command. The imports of commodities will thus exceed the exports, and the exchange, in language which has survived from the days of the Mercantile System, will become "unfavourable" to the countries of the mines, and "favourable" to those which have sent the increased imports. On this account, therefore, there will be a tendency for the precious metals to leave the countries of the mines and to flow to the countries from which the increased imports have come. The same process will take place in the countries to which the precious metals go. There, too, prices will rise, and the value of the metals fall. There, too, a tendency to an increase of imports, and a diminution of exports, will set the balance of trade against the countries and in favour of those from which the increased imports come. There, too, this tendency will result in an efflux of the precious metals. And so, gradually, from country to country the new supplies will pass until they have raised the general level of prices; but the rise will not be immediate or uniform or universal.

Such is the general economic theory of the international distribution of money. The effects of expansion, or, in the reverse circumstances, of contraction, are gradually propagated from country to country. An analogous process takes place within the limits of each separate country. District by district and trade by trade the rise or fall of prices may be traced. The change is not immediate, or uniform, or universal. Just as the new supplies pass in the first instance into those countries which have the largest commercial dealings with the countries of the mines, so they affect primarily the prices of those commodities for which the countries of the mines feel a demand, and they raise the profits of those who trade in them. These traders, being encouraged by the rise, are eager to extend their business, and are ready to buy more largely of other trades. They therefore offer higher wages to their workmen, and higher prices to those who furnish them with machinery or with materials, or supply the commodities on which they, or their workmen, spend their incomes. And so from trade to trade the influence of the increase in the precious metals passes on. Of particular phases, which this movement may present, we shall have more to say later; we may now be content to show its general character and to emphasise the fact that it is not immediate, or uniform, or universal.

The question, however, presents itself whether a rise or a fall of prices, operating in this manner, is the more conducive to general progress and prosperity. In considering this debated problem, we must keep constantly before our minds two facts in particular to which recent inquiry has tended to give an added prominence. One is the powerful influence of the imagination as an economic factor. The older economists have been often blamed for reasoning about men and women as if they were bales of cloth or bushels of wheat, and destitute of feeling. This has, for example, it is argued, led them to exaggerate in their speculative theories the mobility of labour, and to under-estimate the strength of the objections to a practical policy of *laissez-faire*. But, while a failure to accord due recognition to the varying sympathies and antipathies of men and women is thought to have exercised a prejudicial influence on their theory of wages, it has generally been held that no such defect attaches to their theory of money. Indeed it has been aptly argued that it was the familiar, but narrow, experience of the dealings transacted in the money market, which betrayed Ricardo and his disciples into the errors and omissions of their treatment of the human factors of production.[1] No doubt the mobility of money has often baffled the efforts of legislators, who have tried to detain it by main force in a particular country. No doubt it does persistently —we may almost say instinctively—seek the best market, the place, that is, where it will command the highest purchasing-power. No doubt it might seem as if such a human weakness as the imagination might be safely disregarded in any discussion of in-

[1] *Cf.* Marshall: "Present Position of Economics," secs. 4, 5. "Principles of Economics," 3rd ed., bk. i., ch. iv., secs. 5, 6.

animate money. Yet, as we have noticed, the movement of money is effected, not immediately or uniformly, but only after successive intervals of time and through successive areas of space. A rise or fall of prices is neither instantaneous nor universal. Hence an opportunity is offered for the imagination to exercise its appropriate influence; and he must be a dull or blind observer, who does not realise how a succession of rising prices may kindle the imagination, and encourage enterprise, and how a series of falling prices may produce despondency, if not inertia and despair.

In this connection it seems idle to contend that, when prices have found their level again, the change only means that there are more or less counters in employment than before, and that the real wealth, which consists of the commodities exchanged, is not altered because of an increase or diminution in the number of the counters in which it finds its nominal expression. Nor is it really opportune to suggest that, if one party to a bargain gains, another loses. It may be sound sense to argue that the imagination outruns the reality; but the argument is not unlikely to fall on unresponsive ears. If the influence of the imagination be once granted—and it is difficult to dispute the fact or potency of such an influence—then it would seem to follow in logical sequence that, if economists of the older type were wrong in ignoring the feelings of men and women as affecting their action in the production and distribution of wealth, modern economists may also go astray, if they do not allow the possibility that a stimulus to energy and enterprise in the conduct of business, and to the extension of commercial and industrial activity, may be given by that spur to the imagination which is applied by rising prices.

This influence is at once illustrated and intensified by the presence in modern industry of an agency marvellously delicate and extraordinarily effective. This is the agency of credit. Such importance has been given to it by some writers[1] that they have regarded its fluctuations as incomparably more significant in their effects upon prices than any change in the supplies of the precious metals. To this point we shall return later. Here we are only concerned to argue that credit may be said, in figurative language, to furnish wings to the imagination, and to allow of a higher rise in prices and a more extreme fall than would be possible otherwise.

In his forecast of the course of events, which was likely to follow on the gold discoveries of the middle of this century—a forecast which was remarkable because, proceeding from reasoning of an abstract deductive type, it was substantially confirmed by the independent statistical studies of Jevons,[2] thus affording a happy instance of the verification of speculative prediction by the record of observed fact—Cairnes[3] gave such prominence to the expansive force of credit that he held that in England, where credit was more fully developed, the rise of prices consequent on the influx of the precious metals would be far more rapid than in those Eastern countries, where credit was sluggish, if it could really be said to possess any

[1] *E.g.*, Lord Farrer.
[2] *Cf.* "Investigations in Currency and Finance," pp. 56, 133.
[3] "Essays in Political Economy," p. 66.

potency at all, and the currencies were less sensitive, and able to absorb larger additional quantities without furnishing any manifest evidence of change. The existence of credit in his opinion increased the sensitiveness of a currency to new supplies of the precious metals; and we may agree with him so far as to affirm that not only does credit illustrate by its very fluctuations the powerful influence of the imagination on the conduct of business, but that, when the original stimulus has been supplied by some other cause, the imagination is furnished by credit with the means of prosecuting its flights beyond what sober unimaginative sense may countenance. Again, we repeat, he must be a dull observer of the motives, which affect the actions of men, if he does not see how potent a factor may be the imagination kindled by a rise or enfeebled by a fall of prices. It is impossible for men at all times to emancipate themselves from the subtle influence of monetary expressions, and whether it be, or be not, a mischievous delusion to forget the commodities, and attach importance to the money by which their value is appraised, it is a delusion which still exercises unquestioned influence on the imagination of men, and through their imagination, on the conduct of their commercial and industrial ventures. A rise of prices quickens the pace and a fall relaxes the energy; and the causes are not the less potent because they work insensibly, and often, perhaps generally, are not consciously present to the minds on which they operate.

The imagination, then, is a factor for which allowance must be made in any comprehensive view of the effects of changes in prices in the modern world. The other fact, which should be borne in mind in such discussions, is the new importance accorded to the function of the employer. It is not necessary to do more here than recall the bare outlines of this modern addition to economic analysis.[1] The distinction drawn between the employer and the capitalist, the emphasis laid upon the position of the former in the centre, so to say, of the industrial world, and the enumeration of the qualities required for a successful discharge of his important functions, are commonplaces familiar to all who have acquainted themselves with recent developments of economic teaching. It is to the employer that the capitalist resorts to lend his capital, and to the employer the labourer goes to offer for hire his labour. He is the pivot on which the industrial order turns. He is the buffer which has to bear the first brunt of industrial disaster. He is the pioneer who has to point the way to industrial success. No doubt it may be easy to magnify his virtues and neglect his defects: and his qualities may often be such as to repel rather than attract. All that we are concerned to recognise is the undeniable fact that he is credited in recent economic writing with a position and functions of paramount importance in the industrial world. But the very qualities of energy and enterprise, which are calculated to promote the effective discharge of his functions as the director of industry, are specially liable to be influenced by the imagination —to be stimulated by rising and depressed by falling prices. Moreover he is generally, if not invariably, a debtor; for under the modern organisation of credit he

[1] *Cf.* Bagehot: "Economic Studies," pp. 52, etc.; Walker: "Wages Question," ch. xiv.

trades with borrowed money. Thus we find combined in modern commerce the powerful influence of the imagination, the elastic force of credit, and the central importance of the employer, as testimony to the beneficial effects of rising, and the enervating and enfeebling consequences of falling prices.

As a debtor, the employer reaps a real benefit from a rise, and sustains a genuine loss by a fall of prices; and it may be established as the first broad distinction between classes, which experience advantage or injury from changes in prices, that debtors are benefited and creditors lose when prices rise, and that the opposite consequences ensue when prices fall. The reasons are obvious. The purchasing-power of money is in the first case less when the debt is repaid than when it was contracted, while in the second the purchasing-power has increased during the existence of the obligation. The repayment, although nominally unaltered, has in reality undergone material change; and, if prices rise, the burden of the obligation diminishes, while it increases if prices fall. It is partly for this reason that an over-issue of inconvertible paper is generally popular, and is often pressed on a willing or unwilling Government, and that the debasement of a currency is sometimes not resented seriously. Both these cases must, however, be distinguished from a rise in prices caused by new supplies of the precious metals; for not only does that rest on a more substantial foundation, but it is also produced by a natural agency. The issue of inconvertible paper is probably destined to be followed by contraction, and, the higher the rise produced, the more painful and calamitous must be the fall when a return is made to specie payments. The debasement of the currency is a deliberate act with dishonest intent. But the rise of prices caused by increased supplies of the precious metals is generally gradual in its operation, is not of itself calculated to produce a corresponding fall, and is free from the reproach of being the conscious act of a fraudulent debtor. It does, however, undoubtedly reduce the burden of debt, public or private, while a fall of prices as unquestionably adds to that burden. In a modern state the nation, by its representative, the Government, benefits by the insensible reduction of the public debt, and, so far as the security for it is held by foreigners, the nation as a whole shares in the advantage without detracting loss, while, to the extent to which it is held within the country itself, the State gains, and the individual holders lose. Similar considerations apply to private indebtedness, and we are therefore led to consider of what classes in a community the main body of debtors and of creditors respectively consists.

On the one hand, there can be no doubt that among the debtors are some, such as widows and orphans, the physically disabled or the sick, who cannot work for themselves, and depend on the provision made in the form of interest on investments. But among their number, also, are those who will not work, and prefer to live on wealth inherited from a past generation. In the other class—that of the debtors—we find the employers of industry; and, if their function be in reality as important as we have seen that modern economists consider it, if in truth they supply the motive force and the directing guidance to the industrial machine, then a benefit to them is likely to result in general advantage, and a loss will probably occasion general injury. It is true that they may be unduly encouraged, and a wave of speculation may follow on a rise of prices, while a fall may accompany the return of trade to a sounder condition. But, in spite of such considerations, on a broad view of the case, the debtors may not inaccurately be said to represent the active enterprising classes engaged in the production of fresh wealth, and the creditors to comprise the inactive, unindustrious classes living on the wealth created in the past. If a progressive community be one where industry is prospering, and accumulation of fresh wealth is continuous and rapid, then a rise of prices would seem to be beneficial, and a fall injurious, though it must not be forgotten that it is conceivable that a larger quantity of wealth may be wasted in a period of speculative fever than that which is slowly but steadily saved in a period of quiescence, if not of depression. On the whole, however, the balance of advantage would appear to incline in favour of a gentle rise of prices.

It is in connection with the use of money as a standard of deferred payments that changes in prices exercise these effects on debtors and creditors respectively. But in a civilised society there are also a number of fixed payments which are yet not of the nature of a debt; and fluctuations in prices must of necessity affect the real position of the persons making or receiving these payments. Even where they undergo adjustment, the process may occupy a longer or shorter period, and during the interval one or the other party, as the case may be, will experience gain or loss.

In considering, therefore, the comparative effects on the general welfare of a rise or a fall of prices, caused by an expansion or contraction of the supplies of the precious metals, it is needful to frame some conception[1] of the number and importance of those classes, whose receipts and payments are variable, and will adjust themselves with ease and rapidity to the altered value of money, and of the classes, whose incomes and expenditure are fixed, and will only submit to adjustment with delay and friction. So far as fixed receipts are balanced by fixed payments, the loss or gain, as the case may be, will be balanced by a corresponding gain or loss. If the value of money rises, and prices fall, the receipts will be more valuable, but so also will be the payments. If, on the other hand, prices rise, the purchasing-power of the fixed receipts will be less, but that of the fixed payments will undergo an equivalent reduction. Again, where both the receipts and the payments are variable, and are easily adjusted, the result of an alteration in the value of money will merely be an increase or diminution in the number of the counters used, and the real position of the parties will be left unaffected, if we set aside the possible influence of the imagination. But in those cases where we find rigidity on the one side, and adjustability on the other, the result of changes in prices may be important for loss or for gain. Those persons, whose incomes are fixed, and expenditure variable, will profit by a fall, and lose by a rise of prices; and those, whose expenditure is rigid, and income flexible, will reap advantage from a rise, and sustain loss by a fall in prices. In the end, no doubt,

[1] For such an estimate cf. Jevons' "Investigations," pp. 80, etc.

a readjustment to altered circumstances may be effected, but during the interval the gains and losses will assuredly be real, and may easily prove to be substantial; while, before the new settlement is reached, a fresh change may have already begun to operate. In fact, as we have noticed, from the conditions of the case it seems practically impossible to attain complete stability.

One great class affected by the opposition of fixed payments to variable receipts, and of variable payments to fixed receipts, consists of those debtors and creditors whom we previously considered. The debtor may be regarded as bound to make a fixed payment to his creditor out of a varying income and the creditor may be treated as enjoying a fixed receipt, from which he has to meet a varying expenditure. Hence it is that debtors gain and creditors lose by a rise of prices, and that a fall reverses the position. Hence, too, it is that the employers, who trade on borrowed money, apart entirely from the powerful stimulus to the imagination afforded by a rise of prices, and from the benumbing and dispiriting influence exercised by a fall, do sustain a real loss, and reap a substantial benefit, in the two cases respectively. Their profits represent a margin of varying receipts over expenditure, which is by comparison fixed for the time at least, and this margin is swept away by a fall and enlarged by a rise of prices. Hence, too, the agricultural landlord, whose rents, as Sir Robert Giffen has recently pointed out in evidence before the Commission on Agriculture,[1] are in a sense a "margin of a margin," and under the system of yearly tenancies,

[1] Cf. Report, q. 18,160.

which is now prevalent in English agriculture, are altered with comparative rapidity, while the various obligations on the estate, for interest on mortgage debt, or for the provision of dowers for widows or allowances for younger children, are only changed with difficulty after an interval of time, suffers, perhaps, more severely from a fall of prices than the employer, who is constantly paying off old debt and contracting new, and is able, though not without friction and delay, to procure a change in the terms on which he borrows, and, with longer delay and more considerable friction, an alteration in the rate of wages that he pays. A "margin of a margin" is more precarious and liable to disappear before an increase in the value of money; and historical evidence certainly goes some way to show that the agricultural interest is specially likely to prosper when prices are rising, and to be depressed when they are falling. It is true that both landlord and farmer may, like employers, experience a gain so far as their expenditure is variable and their receipts are fixed, and they may find it difficult to take due account of this compensating advantage, as the effects may not be so obvious and immediate. But, so far as their receipts are variable and their expenditure is fixed, they cannot rid themselves of loss; and the subtle and powerful influence exerted by the imagination will increase their sensibility to injury which is more manifest and more immediate. In the contrary supposition of a rise of prices their feelings, as their real position, will be reversed.

In partial opposition to the classes, which we have been considering, and may roughly describe as the directors of agricultural and industrial production, we may set the earners of wages. Here readjustment will, no doubt, be effected in time, and receipts and expenditure may both be regarded as variable in the long run; but the alteration in the receipts may follow after, and lag behind, that in the payments. To all such readjustment of incomes the *vis inertiæ* of custom opposes delay and hindrance, and it is a well-attested fact of economic experience that prices change with more rapidity than wages. It is, then, broadly true that wage-earners are for an interval in the position of those, whose receipts are fixed, and whose expenditure is variable, and therefore they are advantaged by a fall, and injured by a rise, in prices. No doubt, if, as prices rise, they become sensible that their wages are losing part of their purchasing-power when exchanged for commodities, they will demand and insist on an advance of wages. No doubt also, if prices fall, employers will in the end be compelled to claim a reduction. But in either case the adjustment is not likely to be immediate; and it may engender friction and beget discontent on the one side or the other. This delay and uncertainty it is which sweeps away the margin of profit from the employer, and the margin of a margin from the landlord in times when the value of money is increasing; and, were it not for the *vis inertiæ* thus resisting readjustment, the prejudicial influence of a fall of prices would be robbed of much of its injurious effects on the continued and extended production of wealth.

The nice question, however, arises whether, granting the existence of this *vis inertiæ*, a rise or a fall of prices is likely in the long run to result in greater loss or gain to the wage-earner; and it may be plausibly contended that in the case of a rise, although his wages may not respond at once to changes in prices, and for the time he may lose, yet the general air of prosperity, which accompanies the rise, and the encouragement, which it affords to the employer, are not unlikely to enable the workmen to insist more easily on better terms, and to make the employer more ready to respond to a demand for an advance in wages; and that with more rapidity than in the opposite case of a fall of prices the readjustment will be effected. In short, the accompanying friction and irritation are likely, it may be argued, to be less protracted and extensive in the case of a rise than in that of a fall of prices. When prices rise the workmen are more quick to recognise the change, and the circumstances of the times allow them more easily to obtain their object. When prices fall, the change itself is less manifest, the workmen are less sensible of the alteration, and more inclined to oppose a readjustment. Certain cogent considerations may, it is true, be held to favour the view that the wage-earner stands to lose by a rise and to gain by a fall in prices; but such a conclusion is on the surface, and it is possible that deeper considerations lie beneath.

If the readjustment takes a longer time, and is accomplished at a greater expense of friction and irritation, it is likely to impose a more injurious check on production; and on the amount of production the remuneration of the wage-earner must in the long run depend. The temporary advantage, which he secures in the distribution of wealth, is likely, if economic speculation be correct, to be dearly purchased by the prejudicial influence exerted on production, and he will lose eventually in curtailed production, even if he avoids a decline of wages for the time.

The cogency of this argument derives additional strength from a consideration of some tendencies of recent economic progress. Competent observers[1] agree in the opinion that the direction of economic forces inclines in favour of the workman rather than the employer. The trend of public opinion, the removal of legal hindrance, and the support of legal protection, and the power obtained by combination, tend to secure for the workman an increasing share in the distribution of wealth. If the inclination of economic forces be thus correctly indicated, we should expect the real remuneration of the workman to advance; and such an expectation carries with it the conclusion that, when the purchasing-power of money is steady, and prices are unaltered, wages should increase; that, when prices are falling, and the purchasing-power of money is rising, wages should remain steady; and that when the purchasing-power of money is falling, and prices are rising, wages should advance to a greater extent than the rise of prices. If, then, we allow any place for the imagination, it seems scarcely possible to doubt that the workmen will be less sensible of an improvement in their position when prices are falling than when they are rising, and that employers will feel more gradually the burden of the altered distribution when prices are rising, and that when prices are falling they will deem the burden heavier.

---

[1] *Cf.* Giffen: "Essays in Finance," second series, x., xi; P. Leroy-Beaulieu: "Essai sur la Répartition des Richesses," chapters xiv., etc.; E. Atkinson: "Distribution of Products."

They will do so because the surrounding atmosphere is depressing, while the invigorating influence of rising prices stimulates to new exertions; and it seems not improbable that the concealment of the real advance of wages by a fall of prices may prevent them from recognising the change as soon as they otherwise would, and making their arrangements accordingly. These feelings may contain an ingredient of unreasoning fancy, but they do not on that account cease to be potent; and, whether we look at the effects on the conduct and attitude of masters or of men, the conclusion seems inevitable that the beneficial results of such a real change in distribution are lessened, and the injurious consequences heightened, by a fall in prices, which, obscuring the facts to the vision of both parties, minimises the advantage to the men and intensifies the apparent disadvantage to the masters. In other words, the friction, which can hardly be avoided, is increased; and some prejudicial influence cannot fail to be exerted on the production of wealth, which is the only ultimate source and final means of an improved distribution. The energies and efforts of employers are relaxed, and the stimulus to fresh exertion on the part of the men, which, furnished by rising wages, might produce some compensatory effect on the total production, runs a risk of never being applied or felt. On a broad general view of the circumstances, here again, economic inquiry leads to the conclusion that a rise of prices is more likely than a fall to result in a balance of benefit to the whole community. That prices should remain absolutely stable is a fond vision rather than a practical possibility; and, if some movement be inevitable, expediency appears to dictate that it should, if possible, be that of a rise and not of a fall.

There are, however, other classes of the community besides employers and wage-earners, of whose position account must be taken in any estimate of comparative loss and gain. Employers and workmen deserve the most prominent place in such an estimate because they constitute so large a proportion of the whole community; and, their receipts and expenditure being neither rigidly fixed, nor yet entirely variable, the effects of an alteration in prices upon their position are not obvious or easy to appraise. But there are other classes whose incomes are fixed more rigidly. Attention has already been directed to the claims of debtors and creditors generally; and the conclusion has been reached that, in spite of the loss occasioned by rising prices to widow or orphan, or to crippled or sick, and in spite of the comparative absence of speculation, and the more steady, if more gradual, accumulation of wealth in periods of falling prices, yet, on a broad view, creditors would seem to represent those who are living on the results of past accumulation, and debtors those who, by their active exertions, are contributing to the production of fresh wealth, and that therefore a period of rising prices seems to be more calculated than a period of falling prices to advance the general prosperity of the whole community.

This conclusion may not meet with universal acceptance, and it cannot be denied that some cogent arguments may be advanced against it; but it rests on the support of high economic authority. We may now inquire with more detail into the particular classes embraced under the respective designations of debtors and creditors.

An exhaustive enumeration of these classes is contained in Jevons' pamphlet on "A Serious Fall in the Value of Gold";[1] and from his list we may select some illustrative types. The debtors may possibly be governments, or public companies, or private individuals. The creditors may have money in the funds. They may hold bonds or shares in some public company, or they may have advanced capital to private individuals by way of mortgage or by some other form of loan. They may be bankers or money-lenders, or they may themselves have deposits in banks, or friendly, or building, or insurance societies. They will suffer by a rise of prices and benefit by a fall, if the interest, which they receive, is a fixed payment. If they be holders of the funds, the Government, which may be said to represent the mass of the community, will secure a gain broadly corresponding to their loss, or bear the burden of a loss broadly corresponding to their gain. If they be bondholders, their loss may result in an increased dividend for the ordinary shareholders. If they be mortgagees, the property, on which they hold a lien, will reap an advantage, or sustain a disadvantage, which will be in general accordance with their loss or gain.

To these classes of creditors, in the enjoyment of fixed interest, must be added, as the recipients of fixed incomes, public servants and officials, whose stipends are invariable; and their loss by rising, and gain by falling, prices cannot be denied, although it is conceivable that their apparent interest at the moment

[1] *Cf.* "Investigations," ii., ch. iv., secs. xxvii., xxviii.

may conflict with what might, if they only knew it, be their real interest in the future. For their remuneration ultimately depends on the general prosperity of the community, and is therefore finally affected by whatever tends to advance or hinder general progress. Yet it cannot be doubted that the immediate interest of the moment is likely to outweigh in their estimation any such problematic consequences of the future; and that a reasonable regard for their own advantage would lead them to approve of falling, and to suspect the influence of rising prices.

Another class is distinguished by Jevons as comprising those who "are dependent on fixed charges established by law, custom, or convention;" and here it is conceivable that any loss or gain ensuing on a change in the purchasing-power of money may be followed by augmented or diminished business, which may exercise some counteracting influence on the total income. Barristers and solicitors, doctors and dentists, the proprietors of theatres and the organisers of other forms of public entertainment, the recipients of subscriptions, fees, and pew rents, will, Jevons thinks, gain by a fall and lose by a rise in prices without much compensating counterbalance. But tolls on roads and bridges, gas and water charges, fares and rates on railways, payments to porters, carriers, and the post-office, are fixed by law, by custom or convention, and will, no doubt, tend to remain unaltered in their nominal expression, and yet their liability to a real increase or diminution in command over commodities will be largely neutralised by diminished or augmented custom. The loss resulting from a rise of prices to these forms of income is likely to be partial; and the general public, spending more of its income on such items of expenditure as conveyance and amusement, gains in comfort and in recreation; while in the opposite case of falling prices the general public practises a necessary but disagreeable economy, and diminishes the gain, which might otherwise accrue to these special forms of income. In the case of these payments the balance of general advantage seems to lie on the side of rising prices.

Nor in that of public servants and officials, of annuitants and pensioners, is the rise of prices without compensation of a more immediate character than that which was previously indicated. For the resultant hardship is mitigated by the general tendency of economic progress, and this tendency is likely to be accelerated rather than retarded by a rise in prices. There is a general tendency to diminution in the cost of manufacture; and we may perhaps go further and affirm that a tendency is manifest to a diminution in the general cost of production of commodities. Man is ever gaining greater control over the forces of nature. He is continually winning more fruitful results at a less expenditure of labour. Economists now generally conceive the law of diminishing returns as yielding in predominance to that of increasing returns,[1] though each may have its special sphere of operation in which it is more conspicuously prominent; and economic history is usually interpreted

[1] *Cf.* Nicholson's "Principles of Political Economy," bk. i., ch. x. Marshall's "Principles," bk. iv., ch. xiii.: Hearn's "Plutology," ch. vi.

as a record of progress, not of retrogression. For these reasons, at a time of rising prices occasioned by some increase in the supplies of the precious metals, the pressure of the rise upon unvarying incomes is partly counterbalanced by the general tendency of the cost of manufacture, if not of production as a whole, to diminish, and the recipients of such incomes participate in this general benefit.

Nor does the very rise of prices fail to stimulate increased production, which in its turn, unless a fresh rise previously ensues, will ultimately tend to cause a fall. For this reason Cairnes contended[1] that the gold discoveries of California and Australia, in the middle of the present century, would be followed by an immediate rise in the prices of those manufactures, for which the new gold was exchanged, but that the reaction of increased production would in this case speedily bring about some compensating fall, while in that of raw materials, which would not so readily respond by augmented production to the stimulus of the rise, the rise itself would continue longer, and more especially with animal than with vegetable produce, as the difficulties of increasing production were greater and required a longer interval of time to overcome. As we have noticed, this prediction, based on abstract reasoning, was substantially confirmed by concrete fact; and it is owing to the corrective stimulus, thus shown in varying degrees, that anticipations of the effects of new discoveries of the precious metals on the general level of prices have more often erred by excess than by defect.

[1] "Essays in Political Economy," ii.

A point of greater subtlety, and of far less certainty, is suggested by some speculations. It is doubtful whether the general tendency to a diminution in the cost of production, to which we have drawn attention, can be affirmed to the same extent of the precious metals as of other commodities. On the one hand, they belong to a class to which the law of diminishing returns peculiarly applies, and the cost of their manufacture into money, as compared with that of obtaining the raw material, is unimportant. On the other hand, they are less liable to destruction, the stock in existence is considerable,[1] and the annual production exerts an influence, which in ordinary times, and as a general rule, may appear by contrast insignificant. Setting these considerations against one another, it might still seem that, unless the total supplies of the precious metals outstripped, or, if that were beyond " the dreams of avarice," kept pace with the improvements in the production of commodities, prices would tend to fall, and the value of the metals themselves to increase. And yet, in the past history of metallic mining, chance, rather than any regular law which can be ascertained, appears to have exercised predominant influence; and recent metallurgical progress renders all prediction doubtful.[2] The known

---

[1] In estimating the effect of changes in the supply of the metals on the value of money, it must not be forgotten that the metals are also used in the arts; and that this use has been calculated in the case of gold to absorb a very large part of the annual addition made in recent years to the supplies.

[2] *E.g.* the discovery of the cyanide process by which the amount of gold obtained from the ore has been largely increased. *Cf.* Walker: "Money, Trade, and Industry," p. 64, for the part played by chance.

world is, it is true, more accurately surveyed, and the area of unknown regions is rapidly shrinking. Fresh discoveries of the metals become daily more improbable, at any rate on any considerable extent; and the direction of existing mines is more completely subject to the sway of ordinary business motives,[1] on which prediction is less impossible and untrustworthy. Yet the future seems as hard to forecast as the past is to interpret, and the most careful estimate cannot pretend to more than slippery conjecture. It is possible to regard the history of the production of the metals as one of advance and increase, or as one in which new discoveries have formed interludes of more or less brief duration in a steady diminution of supply when compared with a constant growth in demand. It may even be that the future points to a gradual fall of prices in which any rise will be temporary and exceptional. If this be the true interpretation of the economic movement, it would seem to strengthen the force of the opinion, which regards the effects of such interludes as more beneficial than injurious to the general community, and considers that the consequent sufferings of particular classes find sufficient compensation in the broad tendencies of history. But, if the interpretation rest on no firm foundation, the opinion does not fall to the ground; for it is supported by other considerations, which are independent of this particular conception of the economic movement. Those considerations we have endeavoured to

---

[1] One characteristic of recent mining in the Transvaal has been the certainty of the output; and the cyanide process, by making it possible to treat poorer ores successfully, has conduced to this certainty, together with the regularity of the actual deposits.

review, and we have seen that, although in some instances they have allowed and received different interpretations, yet they appear to converge to the broad conclusion that the balance of general advantage lies on the side of rising rather than of falling prices. In support of this conclusion the deliberate and emphatic opinion of some weighty authorities[1] might be cited; and perhaps no opinion is more deserving of confidence than that of Jevons, who, in his "Investigations in Currency and Finance," after carefully considering what classes were likely to be advantageously, and what injuriously, affected by the "Serious Fall in the Value of Gold" consequent on the discoveries in California and Australia, arrived at this conclusion :—[2]

"I cannot but agree with Macculloch that, putting out of sight individual cases of hardship, if such exist, a fall in the value of gold must have, and, as I should say, has already a most powerfully beneficial effect. It loosens the country, as nothing else could, from its old bonds of debt and habit. It throws increased rewards before all who are making and acquiring wealth, somewhat at the expense of those who are enjoying acquired wealth. It excites the active and skilful classes of the community to new exertions, and is, to some extent, like a discharge from his debts is to the bankrupt long struggling against his burdens. All this is effected without a breach of national good faith, which nothing could compensate." Such is the deliberate judgment of a sober and competent observer, and the converse of his

---

[1] *Cf.* some of those quoted in Walker's "Money," ch. iv.
[2] "Investigations," p. 96.

language appears to be true about an increase in the value of money occasioned by a contraction in the supplies of the precious metals. To some notable periods of expansion and contraction in those supplies, and of rising and of falling prices, our attention will be directed in the following chapters.

CHAPTER III.

THE RISE OF PRICES CONSEQUENT ON THE DISCOVERY OF AMERICA.

Towards the conclusion of his long chapter upon colonies Adam Smith remarks [1] that "the discovery of America, and that of a passage to the East Indies by the Cape of Good Hope, are the two greatest and most important events recorded in the history of mankind." It would certainly not be easy to overrate their importance in connection with the present inquiry. For the discovery of America was speedily followed by an increase in the supplies of the precious metals of extraordinary proportions, and the trade with the East has, by its absorbent capacities, mitigated more than once the revolution of prices naturally consequent on large discoveries of gold and silver. It is true, as Adam Smith urges in the earlier part of the chapter, that Columbus, expecting to find by sailing west a shorter route to those East Indies, the rich products of which had found their way through Egypt to Europe, was disappointed with the apparent natural poverty of those countries which he discovered, and which have been misnamed the West Indies, and for lack of advantageous animal or vegetable product, turned his attention to their mineral wealth, and brought back to the sovereigns of Castile and Aragon an exaggerated account of its abundance.

[1] Bk. iv., ch. vii.

But this exaggeration produced the effect that was intended; and the Spaniards took possession of the West Indies, nominally with the "pious purpose of converting them to Christianity," but really with the "hope of finding treasures of gold." "All" their "other enterprises in the New World subsequent to those of Columbus," Adam Smith continues, "seem to have been prompted by the same motive. It was the sacred thirst of gold that carried Oieda, Nicuessa, and Vasco Nunez de Balboa to the Isthmus of Darien, that carried Cortez to Mexico, and Almagro and Pizarro to Chili and Peru." "Every Spaniard who sailed to America expected to find an Eldorado. Fortune, too, did upon this what she has done upon very few other occasions; she realised in some measure the extravagant hopes of her votaries, and in the discovery and conquest of Mexico and Peru (of which the one happened about thirty, the other about forty, years after the first expedition of Columbus), she presented them with something not very unlike that profusion of the precious metals which they sought for."

Of these remarkable discoveries, and of their effects upon prices and the welfare of the community, we are now about to treat; and we may begin by noting that in comparison with those later periods, with which we shall deal in subsequent chapters, our task is in some respects simplified, while in others its difficulties are greatly increased.

On the one hand there is no doubt that the augmentation in the supplies of the precious metals, which followed the discovery of the mines of America, was adequate to produce an important change in prices; and the fact that it operated in this manner cannot be said to be seriously questioned. Adam Smith himself, in his digression[1] on the variations in the value of silver, notes about one of the three periods, into which he divides his treatment, that "how various soever may be the opinions of the learned concerning the progress of the value of silver during the first period, they are unanimous concerning it during the second." "The discovery of the abundant mines of America seems to have been the sole cause of" the "diminution in the value of silver in proportion to that of corn," which occurred during this period, covering the years from "about 1570 to about 1640." "It is accounted for accordingly in the same manner by everybody; and there never has been any dispute either about the fact or about the cause of it." It would perhaps be unduly sanguine to say that no writer has since been found to question[2] Adam Smith's positive assertion; but it is safe to affirm that the consensus of economic opinion would broadly endorse his statement.

The relation, too, of the cause to its effect has not, in this early period, to be slowly, painfully, and uncertainly disentangled from the mass of overlying and surrounding facts. The channels of trade, through which the new supplies would find their way, were comparatively few in number, and easily traced. The organisation of commerce and industry was simple, and elaborate systems of credit were generally unknown. We have not, therefore, to strain our vision to detect the secular movement of prices due to variations in the supplies of the precious metals beneath the fluctuations occasioned at more frequent intervals

---

[1] Bk. i., ch. xi., pt. iii.
[2] *Cf.* for such questioning, Schœrnhof, "History of Money and Prices."

by expanding and contracting credit. We have merely to separate this secular movement from passing accidents, such as good and bad seasons affecting corn, and the like. We are not liable to meet on the threshold of our inquiry with the response which, if true, is enough to throw all such investigations into confusion, that the influence of varying credit is so predominant as to allow nothing, or comparatively nothing, for the influence of the precious metals. Nor have we occasion to trouble ourselves seriously about the possibility that paper or credit substitutes for the metals may, by their increase or diminution, meet any change due to diminished or increased production from the mines. The theory of the action of the precious metals upon prices is, in short, immensely simplified when we contrast the circumstances of the earlier with those of the later periods.

On the other hand, we are confronted at almost every turn by a dearth of reliable statistical data. It is only within recent years that the statistics of the annual production from the mines have been brought into satisfactory shape; and for the early period, of which we are treating, we have to be content with more or less tolerable conjectures. Even now the *total* amount of the precious metals existing in the form of coin, or in that of articles of use or ornament, cannot be other than a guess more or less accurately founded. The *annual* consumption in the arts and for industrial purposes can be ascertained by more authoritative estimates, and of the *annual* coinage the most important mints are careful to preserve accounts. But of the import and export of coin and of bullion, of the relative parts played in the conduct of exchange at any particular time by metallic and paper money and credit-instruments, we can at the best obtain but a rough idea; and of the rapidity of circulation, or, in economic phraseology, of the "efficiency" of the money, no reliable conjecture has been, or perhaps can be, formed.[1] Under, therefore, the elaborate system of modern credit, and the extensive developments of modern banking, it may be declared impossible to observe the precise *modus operandi* by which the variations in the supplies of the precious metals come into contact with prices, and the theory of the exact connection is not easy to demonstrate. Although such difficulties do not prevent the establishment of conclusions of sufficient probability and exactitude, they serve to restrain any undue expectation of the information within our reach. But we can carefully observe, and scientifically estimate, the results of our observation, at either end, so to say, of the process. We can obtain statistics of the supplies from the mines, and we have access to reliable measurements of prices.

For the early period it is true that we do not require, even if they were attainable, statistics on the nice problems of the relation of credit to the precious metals on the one side, and, on the other, to prices; but our statistics of the production from the mines are far less reliable and far more scanty, and we are unable to apply, except in a crude form, that mode of

[1] *Cf.* Dr. Soetbeer's "Materialien," evidence before Gold and Silver Commission, and Report of Committee of British Association (1888) on "Statistical Data available for determining the Amount of the Precious Metals in use as Money in the Principal Countries, the Chief Forms in which the Money is employed, and the Amount annually used in the Arts." (Report, 1888, p. 219.)

measuring changes in prices by index numbers, which has recently been subjected, as we have seen, to thorough examination, and has not issued from the process without improvement. The relation, therefore, between the precious metals and prices is in the early period comparatively simple and direct; but statistics of the metals present more frequent and extensive gaps, and the ascertainment of the meaning and measure of prices is less exact. Yet, in spite of the serious deficiency of statistical data, and of the rough character of the calculations made by the writers, on whom we have in the main to rely, the evidence seems adequate to establish the broad characteristics and effects of that great increase in the supplies of the precious metals, which followed the discovery of America.

The authority, who has been most generally quoted for the statistics of the supplies in this early period, is William Jacob, who, at the impulse of Huskisson, undertook an investigation into monetary history, and published his results some half-century ago.[1] His researches extend from the earliest times to those at which he was writing. It is impossible to read his book without being impressed by the zeal with which he accumulated his material, by the evident wish, which animated him, not to exaggerate, and by the apparent soundness of his critical judgment. He certainly produces the impression of a reliable witness so far as the conditions of the times permitted; and, although he attempts to give the value, and not, as a

---

[1] The full title of the book is "An Historical Inquiry into the Production and Consumption of the Precious Metals," by William Jacob, Esq., F.R.S., 1831.

rule, the volume of production, and his figures are exceeded by those of the most prominent modern authority, Dr. Soetbeer,[1] yet his method of handling the question is still deserving of study, and his results, if doubt be felt of their exactitude, are, in many respects, within the limits of probable truth. The consilience, which he reaches by different processes, may perhaps be held to detract from as much as to add to the likelihood of his accuracy.

He estimates [2] the annual production of Spanish America during the quarter of a century between its first discovery and the conquest of Mexico and Peru at something like £52,000 ; and this amount, which, it may be noted, consisted almost entirely of gold, was, he considered, " very small, even if compared with the diminished quantity which then existed in the ancient world." In 1519 Cortez invaded Mexico, and twenty years later Pizarro conquered Peru. Before their conquests mineral wealth had been made to yield its treasures in the two countries, but they improved the production. For the period from 1521 to 1546 Jacob adopts the estimate of Humbolt,[3] whose authority he kept continually before him in framing his own calculations, of an annual production of both gold and silver of £630,000. Thus the total addition to the existing supplies in the fifty-four [4] years since the discovery of America amounted, according to his calculation, to £17,258,000.[5] This sum, contrasted with

[1] In his " Materialien." [2] Chapter xvii.
[3] In his " Political Essay on New Spain," especially bk. iv., ch. xi. He examined the registers of the mints in Spanish America.
[4] Jacob gives sixty-three years.
[5] Jacob gives £17,058,000, by a clerical error in the calculation of the earlier period.

the existing stock anterior to the discovery, which he estimated at thirty-three or thirty-four millions, represented an increase of fifty per cent. The annual production of the European mines at the same time, which he put at about £100,000, was, he considered, nearly counterbalanced by loss occasioned every year by wear and tear to the existing stock. Allowing for similar wear and tear of the American supplies, he put the total quantity in existence in 1546 at about fifty millions. Part of the fresh supplies, he allowed, would be diverted by religious piety to the decoration of churches and images, and part might take the form of gold and silver utensils; but both ecclesiastical treasures and the private possessions of rich nobles were liable to plunder and to conversion into coin to meet the payment of armies.

It was not, however, until 1546, with the discovery of the mines of Potosi, followed in 1557 by the important metallurgical invention of the process of extracting silver by amalgamation produced by the use of mercury,[1] that the mineral wealth of the New World assumed large proportions. The discovery of Potosi, like so much else in the history of the precious metals, which has accordingly been regarded as a lottery, with many blanks and few prizes, was accidentally made, for an Indian hunter, pulling up a shrub, noticed silver hanging about the roots. For the output of the earlier years of this fabulously productive region the evidence was rendered doubtful by the absence of books of account; but the total annual supply from

---

[1] The process was not applied on a large scale until the supply of mercury was increased in 1571 by the working of quicksilver mines in Peru.

America was put by Jacob[1] at £2,100,000 for the fifty-four years from 1546 to the close of the century, and the annual supply of Europe, stimulated to fresh efforts in mining enterprise by rumours of the discoveries across the sea, at £150,000. The aggregate production of the period would thus amount to some £121,000,000; and, by adding this to the fifty millions already in existence in 1546, and deducting for wear and tear, the final result was reached that by the close of the sixteenth century the total stock of gold and silver amounted to some £155,000,000, or nearly five times as much as existed before the discovery of America. From this a deduction was required for consumption in the arts; and the intensity of religious devotion of the Romanist type prevailing in that Spanish peninsula, to which the new supplies would first find their way, would divert a considerable portion to the decoration of churches; while in the Northern countries of Europe, whither the trend of commerce would carry on the precious metals, the progress of the Reformation would tend indeed to check such religious expenditure; but the increase of plate, easily convertible, if expediency demanded, into coin, was attested by trustworthy evidence.

A fresh deduction was due to the trade with the East, which centred at Antwerp. The discovery of the passage round the Cape, which was coupled in importance by Adam Smith[2] with the discovery of America itself, facilitated that trade, and the drain to the East, which afterwards became so familiar and

---

[1] *Cf.* ch. xviii.
[2] *Cf.* the passage quoted above.

influential a factor in the history of the precious
metals and their effects upon prices, had now begun.
Europe was buying from India and China, from
Turkey, Persia and Arabia, and the new silver would
be given in exchange for Eastern merchandise. As
yet, however, the trade was limited and the drain
comparatively small. Jacob estimated the deduction
under this head at a tenth of the total output, but he
was careful to note that precise data were lacking, and
that, as no direct trade was as yet established between
America and the East, the precious metals, which were
finally taken there, would exercise on their way an
influence on European prices.

For the consumption in the arts he allowed, by the
same rough conjecture, a fifth of the total production;
and these deductions brought out the calculation for
the total stock in existence in the form of money at
the close of the sixteenth century to some £113,000,000.
Jacob himself arrived at £130,000,000; but he seems
to reach this figure by omitting in his final calculation
to make the allowance for wear and tear, which he
had previously put at some sixteen or seventeen
millions. It would therefore seem, if his calculations
were correct, to be within the truth to affirm that the
quantity of coin in Europe had certainly been trebled,
and perhaps quadrupled, since the discovery of
America.

Such is the nature of the method pursued by
Jacob; and we may content ourselves with a sum-
mary statement of the results, which he reached for
the two succeeding centuries. Summarising, therefore, his conclusions for the three periods distinguished
in his inquiries, which correspond roughly to the

sixteenth, seventeenth, and eighteenth centuries, the production of the first would appear to be £138,000,000; of the second, £337,000,000; and of the third, some £880,000,000. In the first period an increase would be shown in the coin in Europe of some three hundred per cent., in the second of some hundred and thirty, and in the last of some thirty per cent. As we noticed before, he gives throughout the value, and does not supply particulars of the volume, of production; and there is no apparent means of ascertaining the basis on which he converted the latter to the former, or of the relative value, which he accorded in the process to the two metals respectively. The figures of the most prominent modern authority, Dr. Soetbeer,[1] for the value of the production in the corresponding periods are considerably in excess.

The difference may be partly due to the fact that Dr. Soetbeer in his later edition calculates the relative value of silver to gold according to the estimated—or, for the period subsequent to 1687, the ascertained—ratio; and it is possible, or even probable, that Jacob may have taken throughout the ratio of $15\frac{1}{2}$ to 1, which was true for the close of the period. But, when Dr. Soetbeer's figures are treated on this supposition, to compare them with those of Jacob, they still show a considerable divergence for the earlier periods. Dr. Soetbeer himself admits[2] a discrepancy between his calculations and those of Professor Lexis for the volume of production from South America and Mexico, which amounts for the whole period, from the discovery of

[1] More exactly (1) from 1492 to 1599; (2) from 1599 to 1700; (3) from 1700 to 1809.

[2] *Cf.* "Materialien," part i.

America to the close of the eighteenth century, to some ten million kilograms of silver; and the discrepancy arises, he states, from the circumstance that he allows a higher figure for the output of the Peruvian mines. He points out instructively that in all these earlier estimates, which must, he urges, be taken and not rejected, for want of more accurate data, a tendency to exaggerate is manifest on the one hand, but that, on the other, the wish to evade the tax imposed by the Spanish Government would lead to under-statement. He himself attempts no estimate of the stock in existence before the discovery of America, or of the consumption in the arts during the three centuries, or of the drain to the East at that time; and we are compelled to have recourse to Jacob, and to the authorities from whom he derives his information, on these particular points. Dr. Soetbeer, indeed, considers that Jacob over-estimates the loss by wear and tear, and this would affect his calculation of the stock existing in the world before the discovery of America; for he reaches this sum by dismissing as unimportant the annual additions since the fall of the Roman Empire, and setting them off against the wear and tear of the existing stock. On the whole, we may say that, as a type of the method to be followed in such inquiries, Jacob's investigations have not ceased to deserve attentive study; and, if his figures cannot be safely employed for exact conclusions, it is because they are liable to the common failing of all statistics for the period. They seem generally to be within the mark; but, by underrating the production of the sixteenth, they may lead to exaggeration of the increase in the seventeenth; and, again, by underrating

F

that, to an excessive estimate of the additions made in the eighteenth century, Dr. Soetbeer's figures[1] certainly indicate a lower rate of increase.

These are for the period from the discovery of America to the close of the sixteenth century some two thousand million marks for the gold, and some five thousand million marks for the silver, or a total in English pounds (reckoning twenty marks to the pound) of some £380,000,000 as compared with Jacob's figure of £138,000,000. For the seventeenth century, the figures of Dr. Soetbeer are for both metals £498,617,000 as compared with Jacob's £337,000,000. For the subsequent period to the close of the first decade of the eighteenth century Dr. Soetbeer's figures are some hundred and twenty-six millions in excess of those given by Jacob.

If we turn to Dr. Soetbeer's figures of the volume[2] of production, we shall be able to gauge by additional and more certain tests the increase, which resulted from the discovery of America. Estimated in kilograms of pure metal, the average annual product for the period from the discovery to the conquest of Mexico and Peru is put by him at 5,800 kilograms of gold and 47,000 kilograms of silver. For the subsequent period, which intervened before the mines of Potosi were worked, the annual product of gold apparently increased to 7,160 kilograms, while the annual product of silver was nearly doubled, and amounted to 90,200 kilograms. But this increase was as nothing to that in the output of silver during the sixteen years following the discovery of the mineral

[1] *Cf.* "Materialien," part i.
[2] *Ibid.*

wealth of Potosi. The annual product of silver became 311,600 kilograms, while that of gold was 8,510. From that time onwards the increase was, with some fluctuations, steadily maintained in both metals. But the silver, which had outstripped the gold, preserved its lead, and by the beginning of the seventeenth century the average annual product had reached 422,900 kilograms, while that of gold was 8,520. At the time of the discovery of America, Dr. Soetbeer estimates that the gold amounted to 11 and the silver to 89 per cent. of the total production. From the conquest of Mexico the proportions were altered to 7·4 and 92·6. But by the beginning of the seventeenth century the relative proportions had become 2 and 98. During the course of that century the volume of production of silver diminished, and that of gold increased, until at the close the annual average for the silver amounted to 341,900, and for the gold to 10,765 kilograms, and the respective proportions to 96·9 and 3·1. The new gold produced in Brazil was beginning to exert an effect; and for the period between 1741 and 1760 the annual production of that metal increased to 24,610 kilograms—a maximum from which it fell to 17,778 kilograms for the period between 1801 and 1810. This large increase in the production of gold altered the proportion between the two metals in 1741-60 to 4·4 of gold as compared with 95·6 of silver, although the production of the latter metal had risen to 533,145 kilograms. In the next twenty years there was a further rise to 652,740 kilograms, in the succeeding twenty to 879,060 kilograms, and in the following ten (the period between 1801 and 1810) to 894,150 kilograms. The proportion of the production of gold to that of silver for these three periods was respectively 3·1 to 96·9, 2 to 98, and 1·9 to 98·1.

Summing up, therefore, the results of the whole period from the discovery of America to the first decade of the nineteenth century, we find that at the outset the production of gold was 5,800 kilograms, and of silver 47,000, and that at the close the respective production amounted to 17,778 kilograms of gold and 894,150 kilograms of silver, and that the proportions occupied by the two metals in the total volume had altered from 11 to 89 to 1·9 to 98·1. For the first fifty years, until the discovery of Potosi, the increase, although important, was, by comparison with what was to follow, inconsiderable ; nor was the alteration in the proportionate production of the two metals very great. But the output from Potosi produced an effect in both respects which can only be called revolutionary. The total production increased by a sudden and enormous advance ; and the silver shot ahead of the gold and maintained its superiority until the close of the seventeenth century. Then the supplies of gold from Brazil produced a change in the proportion, and until the middle of the eighteenth century an inclination in this direction continued to be manifest. But after 1760 silver again secured the advantage. The most notable change, however, occurred in the sixteenth century, and the great increase in the output of silver, which marked that period, can only be paralleled by the Californian and Australian discoveries of gold in the present century.

We may now proceed to inquire into the effects upon prices of this enormous increase. That a notable change was manifest is generally admitted; but, as in the nineteenth century, men were slow to recognise the cause, and, as in the nineteenth century also, the effects were not so speedily or extensively evident as superficial reasoning might have led the uninstructed to expect. The mineral wealth issuing from the mines of Potosi, and the other parts of America, had to find its way into the channels of trade before it could exercise its appropriate influence, and during the process it set in motion neutralising forces. Money is unquestionably mobile—more mobile perhaps than any other commodity which forms the subject of economic treatment—but it moves along the highways of business, and the agents, on whose actions it operates, are not merely receptive and passive. Accordingly, some time may elapse before the effects of alteration in the supplies are generally felt, even when the change itself is great, and, after no long interval, those effects may themselves be merged in the new forces called into activity. For this reason broad conclusions are alone possible in such an inquiry as that in which we are engaged; and, to discern the operation of the cause, we must form a comprehensive view of the effects. The cause works in most cases so subtly, so gradually, and so insensibly, that men, accustomed from force of habit and imagination to regard that by which they measure the value of other commodities as itself immutable, find a difficulty in detecting and gauging the changes which from time to time undoubtedly occur. It is only when they look back over an interval that they can discern what has happened, and, before they can place themselves at a sufficient distance from the phenomena, it is not unlikely that the increased commercial activity, which may follow on an augmented supply of the precious metals, may conceal and neutralise the real influence exerted on prices.[1] To these considerations must be added the circumstance that a previous increase in the supplies itself diminishes the relative effects of a subsequent increase. The percentage of the increase declines; and few more treacherous pitfalls await the tyro in statistics than those which lie beneath arguments from percentages, for he should always take account of the amount on which the percentage is reckoned.[2]

It might seem as if many of these considerations would not apply to the period following the discovery of America. The modern world was then comparatively young and unsophisticated. The organisation of trade was simple. The relation of the precious metals to prices was, by contrast with later elaborations of credit and banking, direct. The addition to the supplies was at once enormous and rapid. The stock of the precious metals existing in the world was admittedly small. Apparently it had not materially increased since the fall of the Roman Empire, and, among the many rival explanations of that fall, all of which probably contributed their quota, and none can, on a sober view, be treated as exclusive, the neglect into which the mines formerly worked had been allowed to fall, and the consequent decrease of money and decline of prices, have sometimes been assigned a prominent place.[3] The extraordinarily abundant out-

[1] *Cf.* Newmarch in Tooke and Newmarch's "History of Prices," vol. vi., app. ii.
[2] *Cf.* "History of Prices," vol. vi., pt. vii., sec. 3, pp. 151, 152.
[3] By historians like Sir Archibald Alison.

put from Potosi consisted of silver, which occupied at that time the predominant position in the currencies of Europe; for it was at once the standard and the chief medium of exchange. Nor was the volume of trade, on which the new supplies would exert their influence, of large extent when measured by later figures. The drain to the East undoubtedly became before long a potent factor, but it was as yet at the very commencement of its future greatness; and the consumption in the arts, which was, no doubt, rapidly stimulated by the growing cheapness of the metals, at the time of the discovery of America was comparatively inconsiderable.

Yet "in England" Adam Smith considered[1] that the new supplies did not produce "any very sensible effect upon the prices of things" "till after 1570"; and he held the opinion that "between 1630 and 1640, or about 1636, the effect of the discovery of the mines of America in reducing the value of silver appears to have been completed." The reasons, on which he founded this opinion, still deserve study; and his whole "digression concerning the variations in the value of silver"[2] is marked by that saving commonsense, that natural acuteness, and that marvellous anticipation of points considered essential by later inquirers,[3] which are, perhaps, his prevailing characteristics. Taking the variations in the price of corn as a standard by which to measure the changes

[1] "Wealth of Nations," bk. i., ch. xi., pt. iii.
[2] *Ibid.*
[3] His conclusions on particular points have indeed been questioned by subsequent writers; but the broad outlines of his inquiry have been generally confirmed; and, as an example of the method to be pursued, his treatment may be said to be unchallenged.

in the value of silver, he concluded that during the first of the three periods of which he treats—that before 1570—the value of silver was rising and the price of corn was falling; that during the second period—that extending from 1570 to 1630 or 1640—there was no "dispute either about the fact, or about the cause," of the diminution in the value of silver in proportion to that of corn; and that during the third period—that between the middle of the seventeenth century and the time at which he was writing—although the "best opinion," which he could "form upon" the subject, "scarce, perhaps," deserved "the name of belief," yet the value of silver seemed to have risen in proportion to that of corn. Such is his general conclusion; and later inquirers may derive instruction from the reasons, which he adduces for selecting his standard of comparison, from the motives, which led him to reject certain prices as evidence and to accept others, and from his criticism of the theories put forward by the writers with whom he conflicts.

That the value of corn might be taken as approximating to the value of labour, which was in his opinion the real measure of value, because, whatever the stage of improvement, the increase in the productive powers of labour would be counterbalanced by the increase in the price of cattle, "the principal instruments of agriculture," and, unlike other forms of rude produce, corn constituted in civilised countries the chief part of the labourer's subsistence, and its supply, being the product of human industry, could be more exactly adapted to the demand than that of those other forms of rude produce—these arguments may not resist hostile criticism, although they contain elements of truth, and they may be dismissed as part of the peculiar apparatus of Adam Smith's reasoning. The preference, however, of the prices of corn to those of labour, because the latter "can scarce ever be known with any degree of exactness," and the selection of prices mentioned accidentally, or in statutes of the realm, rather than those which historians have recorded on account of "their extraordinary dearness or cheapness,"[1] are lessons in the method of statistics. Nor are the answers returned to the upholders of views opposed to his own on the interpretation of the first and the last of his three periods uninstructive.

In the first period he charges them with error due to misleading facts and mistaken theory. In ascertaining their prices they had adopted for the beginning of the period lower prices than those which represented the real condition, and hence they thought that the value of silver was falling and that prices were rising. For instance they—and Bishop Fleetwood among them—had taken the "conversion price," which was the price in Scotland at which a landlord, receiving his rent in kind, might stipulate that he should be at liberty to substitute a money-payment, and therefore, before the average price of grain was fixed at the annual fiars according to the actual market

[1] It may be noticed that Bishop Fleetwood regarded the accounts of Colleges as the "most sure guides," because in contrast with "general histories," "which do mostly give us the prices of things, which are extraordinary, either for cheapness or for dearness," they "delivered faithfully the ordinary and common price of most commodities and provisions," and he thought that the "gentlemen of each university" might, if they would, mend or add to his own statements. (*Cf.* Preface to "Chronicon Preciosum.")

price,[1] was generally, in the interests of the tenants, below that price. Or, again, the statutes of assize, fixing the price of bread and ale, on which they relied in some cases, generally began with the lowest, and worked up to the higher, prices of wheat and barley, and lazy or careless copyists might content themselves with transcribing only the first three or four prices. Or, once more, owing to the turbulent nature of the times, and the difficulty of communication, the price of corn might vary widely from one district to another, and very low prices might be recorded, which might lead the inquirer to infer that the ordinary price then was as much below what it was later as the lowest price of the earlier was below the lowest price of the later period. In all these ways error might creep in to vitiate statistical comparison.

The erroneous theory, which Adam Smith rejected, held that, as with the growth of the country the quantity of silver in it increased, its value would fall. To this he replied that such an increase in any particular country, apart from augmented production from the mines, merely implied, in later economic phraseology, a change in the "territorial distribution" of money. As the wealth of the country became greater, and the volume of its trade increased, more money would be needed for the work of exchange, and, under a system of "natural liberty," without

---

[1] Adam Smith notices that "Fleetwood acknowledges, upon one occasion, that he had made this mistake." "As," he continues, "he wrote his book, however, for a particular purpose, he does not think proper to make this acknowledgment till after transcribing this conversion price fifteen times."

lowering its value by becoming relatively abundant, silver would "naturally seek the market" where it would obtain the "best price"—the largest quantity, that is, of commodities in exchange.

The same theory was used as an explanation of the course of events in Adam Smith's third period; and he met it with the same objection. He allowed, however, that during the earlier portion of this period the price of corn was slightly dearer; but he accounted for this by circumstances affecting the corn and not the silver, and by the difference caused by debasement of the silver coin due to "clipping and wearing." To the difference, indeed, between nominal and real value, occasioned by deliberate changes in the coinage, he pays close attention throughout; and it is a point which no such inquiry can neglect without serious risk of error. The other possibility suggested by him of the change being on the side of the corn and not of the silver has occupied no small space in recent controversy; but Adam Smith's method of selecting the prices of a single commodity for comparison, defective as it might be on other grounds, simplified the problem here, for it was easy to detect any unusual variation in the supply of such a single commodity as corn. He himself was inclined to attribute great importance to the bounty granted in 1688, and his arguments have been severely, and not unduly, criticised.[1] But of the influence of the civil war in causing scarcity, and of the series of successive unfavourable seasons, which occurred during the last twelve years of his third period, little doubt can be

[1] *Eg.* by Ricardo: "Principles," ch. xxii.

entertained; and that he was right in making allowance for these circumstances no candid inquirer will dispute.

Nor has later investigation done more than elaborate his account of the causes to which he considers it probable that an increase in the value of silver would be due. The extension of the market for silver in Europe, owing to the general advance in agriculture and manufacture, the growth of population and industry in America itself, which thus presented a new and enlarging market, the drain to the East Indies, and the consumption in the arts, are all taken into account; and by such considerations he reaches his conclusions that until 1570 the value of silver was rising, because the price of a quarter of corn had fallen from four ounces of silver in 1350, or about twenty shillings in the money of his day, to two ounces, or about ten shillings; that in the second period the price of corn rose from two to six or eight ounces, or from ten to thirty or forty shillings, and that therefore the value of silver had fallen, and that in the third and final period the price of corn declined again, and the quarter of wheat, which had averaged thirty-nine shillings between 1621 and 1626 for the best price in the Windsor market, averaged during the first sixty-four years of the eighteenth century about thirty-two shillings.

Compared, therefore, with the price of corn before the time when the new supplies consequent on the discovery of America had begun to exert an influence, the rise, after amounting to 200 or 300 per cent., finally settled about the former percentage. It is curious to note that Sir George Evelyn, in the paper contributed to the Royal Society in 1798,[1] in which he employed for comparison not one commodity only, like Adam Smith, but an index number based on the prices of a few chief articles of agricultural produce, such as butter, cheese, ale, beer, mutton, and wheat, together with horses, oxen, cows, sheep, hogs, geese, hens, and cocks, and on labourer's wages, reached a rise of 400 to 500 per cent. between 1550 and 1795, and of 110 between 1550 and 1670, but he has been severely criticised by Hallam and other writers.

A rise of prices in England amounting to 200 per cent. may with tolerable certainty be taken as within the truth, and the greater part at least of the increase occurred within a hundred years of the discovery of Potosi.[2] At first the new supplies would find their way to Spain; and the ardent pursuit of conquest combined with insatiable lust for the precious metals to divert the attention of the inhabitants of that country from trade and industry. Nor were those "sanguinary laws" prohibiting the exportation of gold and silver, of which Adam Smith speaks[3] in his own day, without their counterpart in earlier times, and the Spanish Government would be anxious to prevent any large share of the new treasure from passing into the hands of other countries. "In the

---

[1] *Cf.* "Philosophical Transactions for 1798," pp. 175, etc. His prices were "derived from respectable authorities." Vicomte d'Avenel, in his recently published investigations, shows a rise of about 200 per cent. between 1500 and 1675 in France.

[2] *Cf.* Cunningham: "Growth of English Industry and Commerce," vol. ii., pp. 13 and 14. Prof. Rogers ("History of Agriculture and Prices," vol. v., Preface) says that by the middle of the seventeenth century general prices reached the level which they retained to the beginning of the last quarter of the eighteenth.

[3] Bk. iv., ch. i.

chief towns of Spain," accordingly, as Cliffe Leslie pointed out,[1] " prices seem to have risen even before the fifteenth century had closed."

But, in spite of "sanguinary laws," the metals would be smuggled abroad, and, if Spain herself did not manufacture, and yet desired the product of the skill and industry of other countries, she would be compelled to procure it by the exchange of the new silver. Her coinage, too, appears to have been excellent,[2] and the Spanish coins, with their full weight of bullion, would be eagerly sought by men accustomed to a worn currency, whether debased of deliberate purpose by governments or clipped by continual transfer from hand to hand, or by the action of bullion "sweaters." The fact that the Netherlands, by reason of the wide variety and diffusion of their trade, occupied a supremacy which passed at a later age to England, would attract to them in the first instance the new supplies of the precious metal, and it was through Antwerp that the drain to the East passed on its way. The preponderance of trade brought to the Netherlands perhaps the bulk of the overflow from Spain; and Cliffe Leslie observes[3] that the "ascent" of prices was "much earlier" there than in England.[4]

England, indeed, was suffering from the evils of a debased currency; and this circumstance, coupled with the large expenditure of the Government on

---

[1] "Essays in Political Economy," 2nd edition, no. xix.
[2] Cf. W. A. Shaw's "History of Currency," pp. 107 and 108.
[3] In the Essay quoted above.
[4] The ascent of prices in France seems to have been contemporaneous with that in England. (Cf. Newmarch in "History of Prices," vol. vi., app. ii., p. 410, and d'Avenel.)

foreign war, would serve to divert the current of the new metal. With the conclusion of peace, however, and the reformation of the coinage under Elizabeth, the new supplies made their entrance, and the natural consequence followed of a rise in prices. Even then, however, as Cliffe Leslie has instructively argued,[1] the rise does not seem to have penetrated to country districts remote from the centres of business. The prices recorded by Adam Smith and others are in the main, if not exclusively, those ruling in commercial resorts, and in the wilds of the country two centuries afterwards[2] prices were still remarkably low.

It is necessary to bear in mind these circumstances when we attempt to gauge the effects of the rise of prices on the general welfare of the English community. The new supplies were of great abundance, and, when once they came into contact with prices, the rise was calculated to bewilder by its comparative rapidity and extent. The effects were apparently circumscribed, and within the sphere of their operation, the necessary readjustment was, it would seem, painfully accomplished. The rise was not so much a slow imperceptible movement, spreading by steady intervals over an extensive area, where its effects would be merged and obscured in the flowing tide of business activity; but its presence seems, by contrast with later times, rather to have been manifested by a series of jumps so spasmodic as to prevent

[1] *Ibid.*
[2] Cliffe Leslie quotes on this point a table compiled by Arthur Young of the comparative prices of provisions at different distances north of London, in which the price of a pound of meat appeared within fifty miles of the capital to be only fourpence or twopence.

instinctive accommodation, and so sudden as to alarm and confound. For these reasons it is at once difficult and hazardous to argue from records of what occurred in the sixteenth century to the probability of what might happen in the nineteenth as the result of changes in prices due to an increase in the monetary supplies.

The former period, however, does so far resemble the latter that in discussing the effects of the new supplies we are beset by difficulties arising from the plurality of causes; and, among the different causes in operation, the increase of money occupied an important, but not an exclusive, place. On the one hand the period was undoubtedly a time of unexampled activity and enterprise. The long sleep of ages was yielding to awakening influences. The discovery of the New World stirred the imaginations of men. The opening of the passage to India round the Cape quickened their speculative impulses. They were ready, and even anxious, for adventures in commerce and industry. Yet it is difficult to dissent from Hume's opinion[1] that "it is certain that, since the discovery of the mines in America, industry has increased in all the nations of Europe, except in the possessors of those mines; and this may be justly ascribed among other reasons to the increase in gold and silver." Nor is it easy to deny the force of Petty's comparison[2] of money to the "fat of the body politic," or of Hume's image[3] of it as the "oil which renders the motion of the wheels" of trade "more

---

[1] Essays, pt. ii., no. iii.
[2] In his Tract "Verbum Sapienti."
[3] In the Essay quoted above.

smooth and easy." If the "remarkable expansion" of Oriental trade, which was declared [1] by Cairnes, who was by no means disposed to over-rate the advantages of rising prices, to be "the most striking commercial fact of the age that followed," was due in part to the discovery of the passage round the Cape, it was also facilitated by the new supplies of money, for the nations of the East were willing to give in exchange for the precious metals their produce and merchandise. The mineral wealth of America, in short, furnished the traders of Europe with a commodity which the East was ready to take in unlimited quantities. If the lethargy of ages was already giving way before the influence of a variety of causes, and the old order was breaking up of itself, it can hardly be doubted that the fresh supplies of the precious metals, partly by firing the ambitions of men with rumours of the wealth of the newly discovered world, partly by encouraging and developing the trade to the East, partly by assisting and stimulating the legitimate growth of commerce, contributed no insignificant element to the movement of affairs.

On the other hand the revolution—for it amounted to nothing less—which was occasioned in prices, was unquestionably attended by considerable suffering. The change seems to have operated in the areas over which it extended with a rapidity that did not permit of gradual and insensible adjustment. It dislocated the mutual relations of men; and, if merchants and traders were benefited, labourers experienced an injury, at least for the time. On this point there does not seem to be any serious dispute; but we must

[1] "Essays in Political Economy," No. iv.

beware of attributing the evil, just as we must be careful to avoid assigning the good, exclusively to the influence of the new supplies of the precious metals. They are only one of several causes. We must remember that the old economy seems to have been dissolving for some while before the new supplies began to exert an appreciable influence, and that perhaps they can only be said to have hastened inevitable change. We must remember in particular that the debasement of the currency had already produced injurious effects.

In a well-known dialogue by W. S., entitled "A Discourse of the Common Weal of this Realme of Englande," emphatic expression was given to the complaints of the times, and, among these, to the serious rise of prices, with its disturbing influence on the relations of various members of society, represented by the personages of the dialogue. The dialogue has been frequently quoted[1] as evidence of the injurious effects of the rise of prices; and it was at one time supposed to have been written in 1581, and to have referred to the suffering consequent on the influx of the new metal from Spanish America. But recent research has carried back the date of the original edition to 1549, and the rise of prices at that time could not have been due to the supposed cause, if Adam Smith was correct in his opinion—and subsequent investigations have tended to confirm his general accuracy—that the first evident traces of the influence of the new supplies could be detected no earlier than 1570. At any rate it is curiously significant that the special references to the "great

[1] *E.g.*, by Cairnes in the Essay quoted above.

plenty of treasure which is walking in these parts of the world," and the "infinite sums of gold and silver which are gathered from the Indies and other countries, and so yearly transferred into these coasts," are contained in the later edition of the dialogue, and do not appear in the earlier. This discovery, which is due[1] to the zeal and industry of a student, whose premature death has been a cause of regret to economic historians, may serve as an instructive warning of the possible reversal of accepted opinions; and in the case before us, if the dialogue is taken as testimony to the prevalence of trouble and confusion, the cause, to which these must be ascribed, is, not the discovery of America and the rise of prices that followed on the influx of the precious metals, but the deliberate debasement of the currency by the Tudor monarchs.

It may be noted that Professor Thorold Rogers, in his "History of Agriculture and Prices,"[2] expressly distinguishes between the comparative rapidity of the rise of prices caused by debasement of the currency and the relatively gradual advance, which might have been expected, in the absence of this provocative influence, to have attended the entrance of the new treasure into English trade.[3] The debasement of the currency served to postpone that entrance; and the

[1] Cf. a notice of Miss Elizabeth Lamond by Dr. Cunningham in *Economic Journal* for December, 1893, vol. iii., no. 12, p. 669.

[2] Vol. iv., p. 736; vol. v., p. 780. He does not think that during the greater part, or perhaps the whole, of the sixteenth century there was any change in general prices beyond that due to debasement of the coinage. (Cf. also "Six Centuries," pp. 343, etc.)

[3] He would apparently put the rise (not due to debasement) at about 200 per cent.

reformation of the coinage under Elizabeth raised a hope, destined to be disappointed, that the evils occasioned by artificial increase of the currency would be removed when the proper corrective had been applied. But the debasement had already produced disorder, which rendered any immediate recovery impossible, and the new supplies of the metals poured in with greater abundance because they had been excluded before, and the influence of the American output was concentrated instead of diffused. The suffering necessarily occasioned seemed the more alarming and hard to endure because it disappointed hopes which had been confidently formed, and dispelled expectations which seemed only reasonable. It can scarcely be doubted that the debasement of the currency accentuated the inevitable consequences of the influx.

Bishop Latimer, again, who has been identified with one of the characters of the dialogue of W. S., spoke not unfrequently in his sermons of the rise of rents, and assailed[1] in one common denunciation "graziers, inclosers, and rent-raisers." There can be no question that the rearing of sheep, and their substitution for tillage, with the consequent diminution in the demand for labour, and the inclosures of the open fields, with the injury which appears to have been wrought to the previous occupants, were stimulated by the high price of wool required for exportation to Flanders. But we must not forget that Latimer himself did not live to witness the Elizabethan recoinage, when the

[1] Latimer, in referring to the rise of prices, was evidently dealing with that caused by the debasement. (*Cf.* Tooke and Newmarch's "History of Prices," vol. vi., p. 371.)

new supplies found an entrance into the circulation; and that the development of the woollen industry and the practice of inclosure had attracted the attention of the Legislature before the conquest of Mexico and Peru. The Elizabethan Poor Law, once more, has been plausibly ascribed[1] to the influence of the new supplies in dislocating industrial relations and causing distress to the labourer, whose remuneration did not rise correspondingly to the advance in prices. But the previous dissolution of the monasteries under Henry the Eighth seems at least to have borne some part in producing this result, although the magnitude of its influence may have been exaggerated.[2] That dissolution itself was but the accompaniment of a general change, by which the labourer, unable, like his modern descendant, to assert his claims to increased remuneration, unless he was ready to put in motion the costly and cumbrous engine of revolt, was only too likely to suffer.[3]

The evil then, like the good of the times, seems to have been due to a number of causes, among which we may give to the new supplies of the precious metals an important, but not an exclusive, position. Their connection, on the one hand, with the growth of the trade to the East is as obvious as is the fact that they were largely responsible for the splendour of the

---

[1] By Jacob and Cairnes.

[2] *Cf.* Ashley: "Economic History," bk. ii., ch. v.

[3] The Statute of Apprentices of 1563 was apparently designed to secure an adjustment of wages to prices. (*Cf.* Cunningham: "Growth of English Industry," ii., 39, 195.) It is doubtful how far the clause empowering the justices to fix wages was actually operative, and the rise of prices, it must be remembered, seems to have been bewildering

Spanish monarchy. Nor can there be serious doubt that the rise of prices occasioned by their influx injured for the time, at least, the English labourer, whose earnings failed to increase accordingly. Nor is it improbable that the difficulties of Charles the First, and the eventful quarrel which followed, were partly due to the increased expenditure of the Court necessarily occasioned by the rise of prices; for Elizabeth, unwilling to burden the nation unduly, had aimed at limiting the revenue demanded from her subjects, and, while the nominal expression of this might remain unchanged, its purchasing-power would, with the rise, undergo serious diminution.[1] On the other hand, the impulse given to extended trade remained when the dislocation to wages had been reduced; and there are certainly grounds for believing with Tooke and Newmarch that "we have the fullest warrant for concluding that any partial inconvenience that might arise from the effect of the American Supplies of the Sixteenth Century in raising prices, was compensated and repaid a hundredfold by the activity, the expansion and vigour which they impressed for more than one generation upon every enterprise, and every act which dignifies human life or increases human happiness."[2]

One other effect, which they produced, must here be briefly noticed. They caused an alteration in the relative value of silver and gold. We have observed before the change in the respective volume of production. At the beginning of the period,[3] when America

---

[1] *Cf.* Cairnes in Essay quoted above.
[2] " History of Prices," vol. vi., app. ii., p. 414.
[3] *Cf.* Dr. Soetbeer's " Materialien," pt. i.

was discovered, the proportion of the gold to the silver in the total output was as 11 to 89. By the close of the sixteenth century it was as 1 to 98. By the close of the succeeding century it had risen to 3 to 96, and by the beginning of the nineteenth century it was again as 1 to 98. Turning from these estimates of the volume to Dr. Soetbeer's calculations of the respective total values of the annual production, we find that at the time of the discovery of America the proportion of the gold to the silver was as 57 to 43, that by the close of the sixteenth century it had sunk to 17 to 82, that by the close of the seventeenth century it was again restored to 32 to 67, and that by the end of the whole period it had fallen once more to 23 to 76. In framing these estimates of the respective values, Dr. Soetbeer converts the volume of silver into its value by taking the estimated, and, for the period since 1687, the recorded ratio of silver to gold of the time. And yet, in spite of the great changes in total volume and value, which we have noted, the ratio only altered[1] from 1 to 10·45 at the commencement to 1 to 11·80 at the close of the sixteenth, to 1 to 15 at the close of the seventeenth, and 1 to 15·63 at the end of the whole period. The change in the relative volume of supply undoubtedly exercised an influence on the market ratio, but the amount of that influence seems to have been by comparison inconsiderable, and the steadiness of the ratio, when contrasted with the extent of the change, is at least a significant fact. On its precise significance we do not propose at this stage of the inquiry to offer an opinion.[2]

[1] *Ibid.*, pt. ii.
[2] *Cf.* below, chapters v., vi.

CHAPTER IV.

THE FALL OF PRICES DURING THE EARLIER PART OF THE NINETEENTH CENTURY.

In attempting to gauge the effects upon prices of the American discoveries of the sixteenth century the inquirer is confronted by a lack of statistical data; but his investigations are rendered more easy by the comparative simplicity and directness of the connection between the cause and the effect. As he approaches to recent times, he can avail himself of fuller and more reliable statistics, but he finds greater uncertainty on the mode of that connection. The facts of the production from the mines are, in spite of some doubt, more exactly ascertained; that scientific instrument for the measurement of changes in general prices, which is known by the name of an index number, can be used; and the records of prices themselves are more abundant and reliable.[1] But, if the statistical material be more copious and trustworthy, the relation of the metals to prices is complicated and obscured. The din of controversy fills the air. The fluctuations

---

[1] Newmarch ("History of Prices," vol. vi., app. ii.) distinguishes thus between different periods in the records of prices:—
  (1.) From 1401 to 1580, when there are only "Casual Quotations" by historians and other writers, such as Eden in England.
  (2.) From 1581 to 1770, when there are "several independent series of Annual Quotations," *e.g.*, the Eton Tables used by Adam Smith.
  (3.) From 1771 to the "present time" (1857), when there are "Official Series of Annual Average Prices, obtained under Legislative Authority," *e.g.*, the official averages in England obtained under the Corn Acts.

of prices are attributed by one party to one cause and by a second to another. Nor is the controversy gratuitous; for the facts are difficult and intricate. The causes are hard to reach, and the effects are not easily traced. We have, no doubt, to take account on the one hand of changes in the supplies of the metals, and, on the other, to measure the alterations of general prices. But the links connecting cause and effect are not obvious or readily fitted together. The growth of industry and commerce, and the interruptions of that growth, the consumption of the metals in the arts, and the drain to the East, are facts of importance, and admit of rough approximate measurement. But the war with France is a factor in the movement of prices during the period of which we are treating, which cannot be neglected; and the suspension of specie payments is an element of the situation, on the precise character and consequences of which an interminable dispute has raged. Such is the atmosphere of doubt and uncertainty into which we are entering.

From this obscurity, however, some conclusions emerge possessing some amount of certainty; and with these we may begin. In the first place, the broad significance of the facts of the supplies of the metals is unmistakable. That the production of America declined in consequence of revolutionary disturbance is notorious; and from the mines of this part of the world the new supplies of the sixteenth century had come, and the large proportion continued to be furnished at the close of the eighteenth.

Jacob estimated [1] the annual production of Spanish and Portuguese America between 1700 and 1810 at

[1] Chapter xxii.

seven millions, while he put the output from Europe and Africa at £853,233. The total output from Spanish America and Brazil in the succeeding twenty years amounted, according to his estimate,[1] to £80,736,768, or a yearly average of some four instead of some seven millions. The population of Potosi alone diminished from 130,000 at the beginning of the revolution to 9,000 in 1826, and the number of stamping-mills at work decreased from 132 to 12. Nor, when once the mines had been disordered, could they readily be restored to their former condition; for machinery was damaged, and adits were choked. To set against this diminution of more than forty per cent. in the annual American supply, there was an increase in the output from the Russian mines of the Ural Mountains, although in parts of Europe, such as Hungary, a decline was evident. The value of the total annual supply of Europe and Asiatic Russia is put by Jacob at £1,250,000; and, adding these figures to the American supply, he reaches the grand total of some five millions as compared with an average for the previous hundred years of eight, thus establishing a decrease of some thirty-seven per cent. The consumption in the arts he estimates[2] to amount to more than five millions, and the drain to the East, which, he states, had diminished, to two; and, allowing for wear and tear, he arrives at the final result that at the end of 1829 the total stock of coin existing in the world was sixty-six millions less than it was at the end of 1809, and amounted to £313,388,560. In this estimate the output from Asia, which he placed[3] at £1,400,000, was not included; but, as he points out, there was gener-

[1] Chapter xxv.   [2] Chapter xxvi.   [3] Chapter xxvii.

ally on balance an excess of import over export of bullion in the Indian and Chinese trade.[1]

Jacob's figures end with 1829; and are stated in values and not in quantities. If we turn to Dr. Soetbeer,[2] we find that for the first four decades of the present century the value of the annual production of the gold and silver together (converting marks into pounds at twenty marks to the pound) was £10,482,650, £6,463,550, £6,059,100, and £8,108,900. With the following decade, in which the Californian discoveries first began to exert an influence, the total increased to £14,506,500, and with the next decade, in which the new wealth of Australia added its forces to those of California, to £35,834,750. The decline between 1810 and 1830 is obvious, and amounts to a percentage of forty as compared with Jacob's thirty-seven. Passing to the separate figures for the gold and the silver respectively, we find that the volume of the gold falls from 17,778 kilograms in 1801-10 to 11,445 in the next decade, and then increases to 14,216 in 1821-30, and to 20,289 in 1831-40. With the next decade it rises to 54,759, and with the succeeding to 199,388. The volume of the silver falls from 894,150 kilograms in 1801-10 to 540,770 in 1811-20, and 460,560 in 1821-30, and then rises to 596,450 in 1831-40. The fall between 1810 and 1830 in the volume of the silver amounts to little less than fifty, and between the first and the second decade of the century to little less than forty per cent. The increased

---

[1] Jacob thought, however, that this diminution in the supplies had, owing to the operation of counteracting causes, exercised very little discernible influence on prices. (Cf. his concluding chapter.)

[2] "Materialien," pt. i.

production of gold for the years from 1821 to 1840 seems to be due to augmented supplies from Russia, where, according to Dr. Soetbeer's separate figures, the annual output grew from 165 kilograms in the first decade of the century to 315 in the second, to 3,375 in the third, and 7,050 in the fourth. But the decline in the total production of gold and silver from 1810 to 1830 is incontestable; and it was not inconsiderable, for it amounted to some forty or fifty per cent. That such a change should produce some effect on prices was probable.

Nor can it be doubted that, to whatever cause the change be due, the index numbers of Jevons and of Mr. Sauerbeck establish a decline in general prices. Mr. Sauerbeck's number rests on a similar basis for the earlier and for the more recent years to which he has applied his calculation.[1] He adopts as his starting-point the average of the years 1867-77 (which, he remarks, is found in the aggregate to agree with the average of the twenty-five years from 1853 to 1877); and, beginning with the average of this decade, he carries his number back to 1818, while, as year by year, or even as month by month, elapses, he brings it down to date. His number, therefore, covers the longest continuous period of any of the best-known varieties. It is now based on the prices of 45 articles. From 1867 to 1872 the number of articles is 44, and from 1846 to 1866 it is 43, while before 1846 it is only 31. But Mr. Sauerbeck states that the descriptions of these 31 articles "correspond as nearly as possible with those since 1846," and therefore the results shown by his number are comparable through-

[1] *Cf.* paper in *Statistical Journal* for June, 1893, quoted above.

out. It exhibits a steady fall from 1818 until the time when the gold discoveries of California and Australia had begun to exert an influence. The highest point reached is in 1818, when the index number is 142—a point, it may be noticed, far above any attained since—and the lowest point for the period, which we are now considering, is 74 in 1849. When the figures are graphically represented, temporary oscillations are shown in an upward and downward direction in the curve of prices, which mark the alternating periods of speculative activity and trade depression; and a more prolonged and decided upward inclination is manifested in the thirties. But the general trend of the curve is as decidedly downwards as it inclined upwards after the gold discoveries of the middle of the century. If the results are averaged for successive decades, the index numbers are for 1818-27, 111; for 1828-37, 93; for 1838-47, 93 again; and for 1848-57, 89; while in the next decade the number rises to 99. The decline in the earlier years is very marked. From 142 in 1818 the number falls to 121 in 1819, to 112 in 1820, to 106 in 1821, and to 101 in 1822. In 1825 it rises to 117, but in the next year it falls to 100, and in 1827 to 97, in 1829 to 93, and in 1830 to 91.

Turning to the inquiry made by Jevons,[1] we discover results which are generally similar; but his investigations are pushed to an earlier date. They begin with 1782 and extend to 1865. His prices are those of about 40 chief commodities, selected for the period from 1782 to 1844 from tables in Tooke and Newmarch's "History," and after the later

[1] *Cf.* "Investigations," Essay iii., "on the Variation of Prices and the Value of the Currency since 1782."

date based on his own calculations made from the *Economist*. The commodities, with some inevitable changes of quotation, are identical throughout, and are generally similar to those contained in Mr. Sauerbeck's calculations. But for his general average Jevons adopts the geometric mean in place of the simpler method of the arithmetic mean pursued by Mr. Sauerbeck, and he starts with the prices of a single year—that of 1782[1]—a course which he allows to be "purely arbitrary," and yet claims to be permissible, if nothing more is sought than a broad view of the direction of the movement of prices over a long period. A single quotation is taken of each commodity for each successive year, and is sometimes based on an average for the year, and sometimes on a mean between the highest and lowest price for March supplied in Tooke's tables, where, as a general rule, the quotations are given quarterly.

Illustrating his results by a curve of prices, Jevons finds, like Mr. Sauerbeck, smaller fluctuations up and down, marking the flow and the ebb of credit, and beneath these temporary changes he detects a general inclination, first (after 1790) upwards to 1809, and then downwards to 1849, when the lowest point is reached. Between 1809 and 1849 prices fell, he observes, in the ratio of 100 to 41, while Mr. Sauerbeck's figures show a fall from 142 in 1818 to 74 in 1849, or some 45 per cent. In accordance with the results indicated by Mr. Sauerbeck's curve, he notes an "elevation of prices" from 1833 to 1843, which he considers can hardly be assigned to the speculative movement alone; and, after 1852, again in accordance with Mr.

[1] This is the first year of Tooke's tables.

Sauerbeck's figures, prices rise, and the rise is permanent. Such are the general results of his investigation; and the broad conclusions on the course of prices during the earlier portion of the present century reached by his index number and by that of Mr. Sauerbeck are not dissimilar. They agree in establishing the fact of a fall of between 40 and 50 per cent.

In order to eliminate minor influences it is necessary to take a comprehensive view over an interval of time; for only thus can we hope to detect that "secular" movement of prices, which is due to changes in the supplies of the precious metals; and it is because index numbers, especially when represented by the graphic method, afford the means for this wide survey, that they are a valuable instrument of scientific inquiry. Before, then, we can form an adequate conception of the real effect on prices of the known diminution in the production of the precious metals during the earlier portion of the nineteenth century, we must note, and discount, the influence of speculative activity issuing in commercial crises. Periodic alterations of expanding and contracting credit may now be treated as unquestioned facts of the modern economic world, whatever may be the ultimate cause to which they should be traced; and Jevons' studies of these passing fluctuations [1] have contributed in no small measure to this result. In the period under review, proceeding backwards from the acknowledged and notorious crisis of 1847, he passes [2] successively to 1837, 1825, 1816, 1805, 1793, and 1783.[3] The great height, therefore, of Mr. Sauerbeck's number in 1818,

---

[1] *Cf.* "Investigations," Essays i., v.-viii.
[2] *Cf.* Essay viii.   [3] *Cf.* also Essay vii.

its rise in 1825 to 117, and its rise again in 1847 to 95, are explicable, so far as they show a deviation from the general trend, as marking periods of unusual business activity followed by periods of comparative distress and stagnation. The elevation of the curve of prices from 1833 to 1843, however, is, in Jevons' opinion, too pronounced to be assigned to speculation alone, although, as he notes, a crisis of severity occurred in the United States in 1837, accompanied by two partial crises in England in 1836 and 1839.[1] Later research has pointed to the connection of this marked movement with the increase of Russian gold, due to discoveries in Siberia in 1830.[2] In 1805, again, the crisis, which actually occurred, was of minor intensity, and the great collapse was not evident until 1810.[3]

But, after allowing for these apparent fluctuations of the credit cycle, a broad movement remains underneath. The steady upward inclination until 1809, and the pronounced trend downwards from 1809 to 1849, must be due to some deeper and more permanent influence. And the same broad movement was evident, as Jevons subsequently showed,[4] if 1849 were taken as the starting-point of the calculation instead of 1782. In view, therefore, of the evidence supplied by the index numbers, in conjunction with the notorious revolutionary disturbances in America,

---

[1] The elevations of prices due to speculation are assigned by Jevons to the years 1796, 1801, 1809, 1814, 1818, 1825, 1836, 1837, 1847.

[2] Following on those in the Ural Mountains in the previous decade.

[3] The crisis of 1810 Jevons acknowledges to constitute an exception to the decennial variation which he endeavours to establish.

[4] *Cf.* Essay iv., being a letter to the *Economist* on the "Depreciation of Gold," written in 1869.

and a known diminution of the supplies of the precious metals, amounting between 1810 and 1840 to some 40 per cent., it is impossible to resist the conclusion that the cause was adequate to produce an effect on prices, that the effect was produced, and that there must have been a connection between the cause and the effect. The broad concomitance of the variations renders improbable a contrary conclusion.

But the exact amount of the effect, which was due to the cause, is less easy—is, indeed, impossible—to determine; and the relation of the cause to the effect is far less obvious than it was in the period treated in the preceding chapter. At that time the influence of credit was comparatively insignificant, and the elaborate organisation, through which it operates in modern commerce, was practically unknown. The crisis of 1793, indeed, has been described as the "first modern crisis."[1] It is true that Jevons has gone far to establish the periodical recurrence of such fluctuations for the whole of the eighteenth century, and the South Sea bubble of 1720 is as notorious as that "Black Friday" of the Overend and Gurney smash, which was separated by an interval of nearly a century and a half. It is true also that the crisis of 1793 may have earned the designation of the "first modern crisis," because it is the first of which the course can be traced with any scientific exactness. But it is certainly noticeable that even its influence, as Jevons has remarked, can scarcely be detected in the general curve of prices, and it is incontestable that the extensive development of banking and credit, with all its

[1] *Cf.* "Investigations," Essay vii.

confusing effects on the relation of the precious metals to prices, accompanied, and did not precede, that industrial revolution, which marked the close of the last and the opening of the present century.

But what, it may be asked, of that revolution itself? Does it not supply a common cause acting on commodities, which renders it unnecessary to look for any other explanation of the fall of prices? It must be admitted without hesitation that the tendency of the times inclined to an improvement in the methods of production, which would naturally result in an increase in the number of commodities and a diminution in their prices. A broad general cause of this description stands, it must be allowed, on a different footing from the assertion that, if each commodity be considered by itself, a sufficient explanation of changes in prices can be discovered without raising the question of any alteration in the supplies of the precious metals. For the very meaning of an average is that minor influences are eliminated and the action of some common cause detected. The validity of an index number rests in the last analysis on the possibility of this elimination; and the advance established by the inquiries of such a writer as Jevons over those of Tooke consists[1] in the greater breadth of view attained. But the confidence, with which minor causes affecting particular commodities can be dismissed by enlarging the basis on which the average of prices rests, and passing influences common to all, such as

[1] *Cf.* paper by Sir Robert Giffen, in *Statistical Journal* for December, 1888 (vol. li., pt. iv.), on "Recent Changes in Prices and Incomes Compared," 757. "To my mind he" (*i e.*, Tooke) "is completely superseded by Jevons."

the ebb and flow of credit, can be discounted by increasing the interval over which the observation extends, may be shaken by the possibility of the presence and action of some general cause common to all, or to a large majority, of the commodities, which is abiding and not transitory. Such a common cause may be found in the general progress of civilisation, if it is the case, as some observers have maintained, that man's efforts to win wealth from bounteous or reluctant nature are, with the lapse of time, rewarded with more success in the case of the mass of commodities than in that of the precious metals. This tendency, however, if real, is so permanent that it may be taken to be always present; and, while it would serve to account for a general downward inclination of the curve of prices, it does not furnish any adequate explanation of the reversal of a movement in the opposite direction. If the general inclination be interrupted by an upward tendency, then, when this tendency is reversed, we require some explanation of the change different from any to be found in the action of that which has been always present. The interruption itself must be due to a different cause, and the cessation of the interruption must be occasioned by the removal or counteraction of that cause.

But it may be argued that this general tendency to progress may be accelerated, and thus outweigh the influence of the interrupting cause. Even then the interrupting factor itself must have grown relatively less potent, and so far it is shown to have been a contributory cause to the previous movement; and, granting the possibility of a relative increase in the general tendency as a cause adequate to produce a fall of prices, we have still to ask whether, as a matter of actual fact, such an increase was manifested in the particular period under consideration. The time, when England was laying the foundations of her manufacturing and trading supremacy, was unquestionably a period of development of business and of growth in population. If the supplies of the precious metals had been maintained at their former level, the work of exchanging, which they would be called upon to discharge, would, in consequence of that manufacturing development, and of the growth of population, and of the number of commodities produced, have undergone a relative increase. The precious metals would, therefore, have tended to rise in value by reason of their relative scarcity; and the monetary expression, or, in other words, the prices of commodities, would have tended to fall in consequence of their relative abundance. That such a cause was in operation during the first portion of the present century, and that the fall in prices between 1810 and 1849 may be attributed to it in part, cannot be doubted. But it is undeniable that the same cause was acting upon prices in the previous period when they were rising. Recent inquiry has modified the conception sometimes formed of the "industrial revolution" and suggested by its very name. It has traced rudimentary beginnings of later developments to earlier times, and substituted the epithets "gradual" and "varied" for "sudden" and "uniform."[1] But, whether or not the designation of "revolution" be mislead-

[1] *Cf.* Hobson's "Evolution of Modern Capitalism," chapter iii., and Taylor's "Modern Factory System," chapters i.-iii.

ing, it is certain that those remarkable inventions, to which the title is largely due, were exerting an influence on the manufacturing development, and that the industrial organisation was undergoing a transforming change, before no less than after the time when the inclination of the curve of prices altered; and it would even seem that the conclusion of peace removed, in some measure at any rate, the stimulus to that development and change, which had been applied in extraordinary potency in England by the absence of competition on the part of those foreign countries that formed the seat of war.

The question, to use the language applied by Sir Robert Giffen to a later period of changes in prices, must be viewed "dynamically."[1] We find that both before and after the change in prices the manufacturing development and the industrial transformation were progressing.[2] Before the change the movement of prices, like that manufacturing and industrial progress, tended in an upward direction; but after the change the two movements diverged, and, while the manufacturing development continued—it might be, after an interval of comparative slackness, at an accelerated rate—the movement of prices altered its direction and inclined downwards. The admitted tendency of the manufacturing development was unquestionably to lower prices; but it cannot be employed as an explanation at once of the rise of prices before and of the fall after, and the presence of some other cause is indicated. Some factor must be found, which was operating before the change, and was then

---

[1] *Cf.* paper quoted above.
[2] Tooke ("History," p. 5) would have concurred in this opinion.

removed, or some fresh cause must be discovered, which then commenced to act. In either case it is to this cause mainly that the logic of the facts would attribute the change.

From an unwillingness to admit the competence of two causes, which were commonly assigned for the rise of prices, followed as it was by the fall, Tooke, in his elaborate investigations [1] of the period, attached the chief importance to the varying seasons. This exclusive emphasis may be traced to a certain narrowness of view,[2] which may perhaps be said to have manifested itself especially in two ways. If short periods of years are taken, the changing seasons may seem, as Tooke contended, to account adequately for fluctuations, even of great extent, in the price of corn and of other forms of agricultural produce; for such commodities belong to a class the demand for which is inelastic and therefore unresponsive to changes in the supply. The rise or fall of price occasioned by some alteration in the supply may appear to be out of all proportion to the nature of the change. But if, unlike Tooke, we extend our survey over longer intervals, the influence of the seasons is generally merged in other causes; and Adam Smith's opinion on the steadiness in the value of corn is, with some qualifications, apposite. Nor would changes in the seasons adequately account [3] for a general rise or fall

---

[1] In his (1838) "History of Prices and of the State of the Circulation from 1793 to 1837" (an enlargement of an earlier work).

[2] *Cf.* Prof. Foxwell in evidence before Commission on Agriculture, qq. 23,580, etc.

[3] Even if we allow for the indirect influence of good or bad harvests on general expenditure.

of prices; and such, as Jevons has urged,[1] was the character of the alterations shown.

The two causes, which Tooke dismissed as insufficient, were the inconvertible paper currency and the war. To both he was inclined to attribute very little influence; and he was certainly successful in showing that to both exaggerated importance had been given. What he attempted to prove seems often to have been this—that, even if it were established that a rise of prices had occurred of a character, which could be plausibly ascribed to the one or the other of these agencies, the change would have taken place in any event, and therefore they could not be considered the cause. To this method of argument he added another, on which later investigation has thrown some doubt. Probably owing to an inability to attain a broad view of the circumstances, he seems to have expected that the presence of the cause and the appearance of the effect would necessarily be coincident, and to have held that, if he could show that the supposed effect was not in its outward manifestation simultaneous with the alleged cause, he had proved the impossibility of their connection. This mode of reasoning appears repeatedly in the course of his inquiries; and, although it is not absent from later investigations, the more scientific knowledge of the conditions of the problem, which has been subsequently gained, has exposed to serious question the reliance, which can be placed upon it. It is true that in dealing with the effects of the war, or of an increase in the issues of

---

[1] "Investigations," p. 131. Tooke is inclined to attribute the changes in the prices of other articles also to circumstances of their own production rather than to any change in the volume of money.

paper money, the expectation that the cause would be followed immediately by the effect was better founded than it would be with respect to the relation to prices of the supplies of the precious metals. But, even thus employed, the method was open to objection.

Less doubt may be felt of Tooke's contention that [1] the increased military expenditure, and the consequent stimulus to demand, meant in many, perhaps in most, cases a transfer from the pockets of one part of the nation to another, and (on the supposition that no alteration occurred in the quantity of the circulating medium) implied a change, not in general prices, but in the relations of the prices of one commodity to those of another. Whether an index number, like that of Jevons or of Mr. Sauerbeck, would be prejudicially affected by such a change, would depend on its comprehensive character; and, unless the commodities, of which it was composed, consisted to a preponderating extent of those, the prices of which were thus specially raised by the war, or of those, the prices of which were similarly lowered, the general change indicated might be treated as independent of this influence. Tooke himself was ready to allow [2] that the war might have obstructed the importation of foreign produce, and have combined with a succession of bad seasons to raise the price of corn; and, on a broad survey of the facts, the war must be pronounced to have exercised an influence on the course of general prices, as measured by an index number. But we may agree with Tooke that, in the case of many of the effects ascribed to it, counteracting influences were

---

[1] *Cf.* pt ii., chap. iii., p. 92.
[2] Chapter vii.

at work, which were competent to neutralise its action, and that in the case of others the effects were manifested in a more pronounced shape, and in fuller measure, during the succeeding peace than during the war itself.

To arrive, then, at a correct decision on the precise influence of the war in raising, and of the subsequent peace, in lowering prices, required a balancing of opposite considerations. But, if in this case the precise result was doubtful, it was, perhaps, more difficult to gauge the exact effects of the other cause which Tooke examined. This was the question of the paper currency.[1] That during the period of the Bank Restriction the inconvertible paper was depreciated, and that prices reckoned in it rose, was a fact established by that Report of the Bullion Committee, which has obtained such classic fame. That the depreciation amounted at the least to the difference between the market and the mint price of gold,[2] and that there were times when the degree thus indicated was no less than twenty-five per cent., is undeniable. But Tooke endeavoured to show—and in this he seems to have been successful—that with brief exceptions during the first twelve years of the war the depreciation was not more than four per cent., and that at the time of the resumption of cash payments it had again

[1] Pts. iii., etc.

[2] Excluding, as the Committee stated (p. 12), a small sum equivalent to the loss of interest incurred in converting bullion into coin, and to the diminution by use in weight of the coin, and to legal impediments to smelting into bullion (none but light coin being allowed), and to exportation (that of our own gold coin or gold produced from our own coin being prohibited). The first of these causes was inoperative after 1797, and the other two would only account for a very small depreciation.

reached that figure. So far as the influence of the Resumption Act of 1819 was concerned, it could not, he argued, be held responsible for a fall in prices of thirty or forty or fifty per cent. The fall below the specie limit of the exchanges formed, indeed, in his opinion, a proof of the depreciation of the paper, and was a test by which to gauge the influence upon prices to be attributed to the inconvertibility and over-issue of the note. But, so far as the effects ascribed to it in promoting the increased use of substitutes for metallic money, in stimulating the issues of the country banks, or in giving a fresh expansive force to credit, were concerned, those influences, he maintained,[1] were equally operative, and were indeed more obviously manifest, after the resumption of cash payments, when prices were falling and not rising. In fact, but for the unusual pressure caused by large foreign payments, prejudicially affecting the exchanges, he does not think [2] that the issues would have proved generally excessive, or more than would have been needed with convertible paper or a purely metallic currency.

It is true that in the subsequent controversy, in which he appears to later students as protagonist on the one side, and opposed to Lord Overstone on the other, the Legislature adopted[3] the view of his opponent on the possible effects of a paper currency in aggravat-

[1] Pt. iii., ch. ii., sec. 2.   [2] Ibid., sec. 4.
[3] In the Bank Charter Act of 1844. It may be added that Tooke himself, in the first edition of his work, agreed with the views afterwards advocated by Lord Overstone, and contested by himself. In one of the prefaces to the later volumes he acknowledges the correctness of the history of the change of his opinions given by another writer.

ing the excesses of speculative excitement, and the probability that, without express provision for maintaining a coincidence between the issues and the changes in the metallic basis on which they rested, the paper, even if convertible in name, might still be issued in excess, and by that excessive issue would exert a mischievous influence on prices. It is true also that a question of some nicety arises on the possibility of the depreciation of the paper against gold failing to afford an exact index of its own depreciation against commodities as compared with that of gold.[1] And once more it is true that here, as in the former case of the war, Tooke, though with more reason, seems to look for an instantaneous connection between the changes in the cause and the corresponding alterations in the effect.

But, after allowing due weight to such considerations he appears to have been successful in disproving[2] the likelihood of any more direct action of the inconvertible paper upon the course of general prices, so far, at least, as the special point with which he was dealing—its inconvertibility—was concerned, than that shown by the difference between the mint and the market price of gold; and in the index numbers both of Jevons[3] and of Mr. Sauerbeck[4] express allowance is made for this amount of difference. Into the mazes, therefore, of the controversy on the precise effects of the suspension and resumption of cash payments, which, begin-

---

[1] *Cf.* Walker : "Money," ch. xvii.
[2] *Cf.*, however, Sumner: "History of American Currency," pp. 253, etc., for qualifications of Tooke's views.
[3] *Cf.* "Investigations," p. 127.
[4] *Cf.* paper in *Statistical Journal* for June, 1893, p. 240.

ning with this period, was prolonged beyond the passing of the Bank Charter Act in 1844, we need not enter further.¹ That the resumption of cash payments was at once necessary and painful, and that, like the subsequent contraction of excessive issues of paper by the country banks, it may, both by its own operation, and by its conjunction with other causes, have tended to engender a feeling of extreme depression, to have increased the normal ebb of the tide of credit, and to have accelerated the fall of prices, may be allowed. But it was perhaps from a failure to detect the other underlying causes that men were inclined to assign to the manipulation of the paper currency such exclusive importance.

The expansion of the paper issues may also have exercised an indirect influence, in which some explanation may be found of the apparent discrepancy shown by experience between depreciation of inconvertible paper measured against gold and its depreciation when contrasted with commodities. The large issues of the Bank of England during the Restriction, and of the country bankers, must, as Jevons has urged,² when taken in conjunction with the paper currencies of France and Austria, of Russia and of other countries, have thrown some quantity of the precious metals on the market, and the natural result would be a rise of prices. Tooke is ready³ to allow the possibility of

---

[1] The question, on which the controversy mainly turned, was the effect of a currency convertible in name, but appeal was constantly made by the disputants to the experience of the Restriction and the Resumption, and the facts of those times were interpreted in opposite ways. Tooke himself was open to the charge of a complete change of opinion. (*Cf.* above, p. 122, note 3.)

[2] "Investigations," 131. [3] "History," pt. iii., ch. ii., sec. 1.

such an effect following on such a cause, but he thinks that at the time of the Bank Restriction opposing forces would more than counterbalance it. The hoarding by governments in their war-chests, and by private individuals alarmed at the disturbance of the times, the obstruction of the familiar channels of commercial intercourse, and the hindrance to business, which would retard the free circulation of money and diminish its "efficiency," and the payments to armies in the field, would thus operate, would combine to raise the demand for money and to lower prices. What the precise result on balance might be it is not easy to say. Tooke himself considered that the amount released from the English circulation, and recovered after the resumption of cash payments, would be small and inappreciable compared with the stock of the metals in existence. Jevons is disposed to concur with Jacob [1] in attributing little influence to the effects of the paper currencies in liberating metal. But it must be remembered that these effects would be increased by according with the natural movement of the metals themselves; and the production of the metals was increasing before the revolutionary disturbances in America, as it was afterwards diminishing, when prices were falling and cash payments were resumed. Some influence may also be attributed to improvements in metallurgy which seem to have been affected at the former time.

A circumstance, on which Tooke relied [2] to prove the unimportance of this liberation of metal from the currency, was the increase in the drain to the East.

---

[1] Chapter xxx.
[2] "History," pt. iii., ch. ii., sec. 1., p. 140.

That, he urged, was an augmented demand which would tend to counteract any addition to the supplies. It is curious to note the different inference drawn by Jevons[1] from the same phenomenon; for he expressly cited the increase in the drain as corroborative evidence of a comparative redundancy in Europe. It is certainly true that in the history of prices the East has on more than one occasion proved the great absorbent of the precious metals. It was so at the discovery of America, when the Netherlands, attracting by their trade the new supplies from Spain, passed on a large portion in exchange for Oriental merchandise.[2] The same phenomenon was repeated at the later period of the discoveries of Californian and Australian gold in the middle of the present century.[3] Again—this time through the channel offered by the compensatory action of the French bimetallic standard—the new gold flowed to the Paris mint, and displaced the silver, which was carried to the East. During the process the prices of Eastern produce were relatively lower than those of the countries from which the new supplies were passing; and, therefore, when Jevons found a similar set of conditions manifested at the period which we are now considering, he drew a similar conclusion, and argued back to the probability of a redundancy in Europe, followed by comparative scarcity. The one implied a rise of prices due to abundance of the monetary medium, the other involved contraction of the monetary supplies with its inevitable consequence of a fall in prices. The facts

[1] "Investigations," pp. 133, etc.
[2] *Cf.* chapter iii.
[3] *Cf.* chapter v.

admitted obviously of such an interpretation; but their meaning must be broadly and not narrowly construed. The prices of Oriental produce were low relatively to those of Western goods when prices in England were at their highest level.[1] The drain to the East was at that time greater than it had been; but after 1819 it declined until for a year or so, about 1832, the balance of trade was actually against India, and the flow of bullion turned outwards. An exact coincidence was not established; for in 1814 prices in Europe had fallen, and those of Oriental produce had risen, while the drain to the East increased.[2] But a broad correspondence was manifest; and the advance of Jevons on Tooke consists largely in the greater attention paid to broad as opposed to narrow considerations.

By eliminating, therefore, other causes, we are brought to the conclusion that the change in the supplies of the precious metals, which unquestionably occurred, must have exercised[3] considerable influence. An important incident of its relation to prices has yet to be noticed. The prices, of which the changes were investigated in the preceding chapter, when the rise consequent on the discovery of America was examined, were silver prices; but the prices, on which the index

---

[1] According to Rogers, this seems to have been also the case in the seventeenth century.

[2] Jevons urges ("Investigations," p. 135) that this "might be accounted for by the opening of markets, and by political events," which might "dislocate and reverse trade for a few years," while "on an average of a long period trade will assert its own character, and deeper causes will produce their effects."

[3] Tooke: "History," pt. iv., ch. xi., sec. 3, allows the possibility of *some* influence.

numbers of Jevons and of Mr. Sauerbeck are based, are given in gold. The history of the metallic currency of this country is one of the topics, which have derived elucidation from the interest aroused by recent controversy; and, although doubt may be felt on points of detail, it does not seem too sanguine to believe that agreement is possible on the main particulars. The chief result of the fresh interest, which has been awakened, may perhaps be thus described. Accepted traditional accounts have been re-examined, and reasons adduced for doubting whether the interpretation commonly given to the language and the acts of those, who set on foot, and carried out, important monetary changes, has not been due to some misreading or misunderstanding of their meaning and purpose by later authorities. It is difficult for men, who live in one environment, to place themselves in the position of those dwelling in another; and it is a common error with students in every branch of knowledge, and with practical men in every department of affairs, to read into the writings and actions of their predecessors a significance and intention characteristic, not of the time in which those predecessors lived and wrote, but of their own later age. The candid critic will allow that the learned researches of the late Mr. Dana Horton,[1] and of others,[2] into the monetary history of the last two hundred years, have at least established a *prima facie* case for reconsidering the interpretation of phrases used by Petty, and Locke, and Newton, which has been handed down through

---

[1] In his "Silver Pound," and other publications.
[2] *E.g.*, Mr. H. H. Gibbs in his "Colloquy on Currency," 3rd edition.

the medium of the writings of Lord Liverpool and the speeches of Sir Robert Peel. Indeed, it may be doubted whether in the study of monetary history an analogue may not be found to the practice, which Bagehot considered [1] characteristic of the economists of his own day, who recognised so completely the supremacy of Mill that they saw in Adam Smith and Ricardo, if they consulted their writings at all, only what he taught them to see, or to an opinion, perhaps still more general, which regards Economics as non-existent before the " Wealth of Nations." Certainly the supremacy enjoyed by Lord Liverpool's "Treatise on the Coins of the Realm" is not unlike that occupied by Mill in Bagehot's description, and inquirers into the history of the currency in England prior to the introduction of a gold monometallic standard are probably even less numerous than researchers into the antecedents of the " Wealth of Nations."

Yet, whatever be the precise interpretation to be given to the policy and opinions of monetary reformers, the main facts of the monetary history of the last two hundred years are established with tolerable completeness. In Adam Smith's time, as at the discovery of America, the silver pound was the monetary unit, and prices were reckoned in silver. "In England," he writes,[2] "and," "I believe," "in all other modern nations of Europe, all accounts are kept, and the value of all goods and of all estates is generally computed in silver." But, while the pound was the unit, the current silver coin was of lower denomination; and, while at first the pound contained a pound

---

[1] " Economic Studies," p. 215.
[2] " Wealth of Nations," bk. i., ch. v.

of metal, and was coined into twenty shillings, and two hundred and forty pence, and therefore the penny also contained a pennyweight, in Adam Smith's time the pound was coined into sixty-two shillings. In addition to silver coins, from the time of Edward the Third,[1] gold also circulated. It was rated at a certain ratio to the silver; and in England, as in continental countries, by altering the terms of purchase of either metal at the mint, or the weight or fineness of the bullion put into the coin, governments seem to have attempted to encourage the influx of the metals from countries where they were rated lower, and to prevent their efflux to countries where they were rated higher.[2] For, in spite of prohibition, bullion exchangers found it profitable to send the metals to a better market, and, where the ratio became more favourable to one or other metal than that prevailing elsewhere, these motives would operate, while their comparative scarcity before the discovery of America increased the desire, and intensified the struggle, to secure and retain possession of them. The natural course of trade and the lack of native coin brought foreign monies into different countries; and the selection of the better coin for export, and deliberate "clipping" by bullion sweaters, together with legitimate and regular wear and tear, tended to cause confusion in a currency, and to render men uncertain of the worth of the money they were handling.

Into such a condition, largely due to deliberate debasement, the English currency had fallen in the reign of Elizabeth, when the first great recoinage was

---

[1] *Cf.* Shaw's "History of Currency," p. 12.
[2] *Ibid., passim.*

effected. By the time of William the Third a similar condition prevailed, and again a reformation of the currency was undertaken.[1] In the interval the principle of free and gratuitous coinage had taken the place of a varying seigniorage; and this important change, which opened a free mint to both metals, was effected in 1666. Between the recoinage of Elizabeth and that of William the silver had remained unaltered, and the gold had been raised four times. The gold coin current was the guinea, which, though legal tender at a value of twenty shillings, was apparently accepted in government offices at twenty-one shillings, and then for some time at twenty-one shillings and sixpence. The silver, by dint of clipping and wearing, and exportation of the heavier coins, deteriorated further, and, in a short space of time, the guinea rose from twenty-two to thirty shillings. In a graphic passage [2] Macaulay has described the evils thus occasioned, when money had lost even that amount of certainty of value, which was necessary to make it a convenient medium of exchange.

The light coin, accordingly, was called in, and new coin issued in its place of the Elizabethan standard; for it was determined to maintain at its old intrinsic value the silver,[3] which was the unit of account. The gold guinea was, therefore, rated to the silver, first at

[1] *Cf.* Dana Horton: "Silver Pound," chapters v., vi.
[2] "History of England," ch. iv.
[3] Mr. Horton contends that insistence on this condition was compatible with what, as a matter of actual fact, existed—the official rating of gold, and free coinage and unlimited legal tender of both metals—and that it cannot be used as a valid argument for monometallism.

twenty-eight shillings, then at twenty-six, and then at twenty-five, until it was brought down at last to twenty-two. The free coinage of gold was suspended for a few months, and the importation of guineas prohibited, while the early stages of the recoinage were carried through. The manner, in which the recoinage affected the position of the guinea, seems to have been of this nature. As legal tender in the fullest sense it was considered to be worth twenty shillings, and, by the provisions connected with the recoinage, it was not to be current for more than twenty-two. In government offices it appears to have passed at this rate, until in 1699 orders were issued to reduce its rating to twenty-one shillings and sixpence. In 1717, in accordance with a report from Sir Isaac Newton, as Master of the Mint, it was reduced to twenty-one shillings, and was to pass current at that rate.

But, both before and after the recoinage, the gold had been rated too high in England as compared with the rate abroad, and the natural result had followed that, under the system of free and gratuitous coinage, it had been poured into the mint, and the silver, underrated by comparison, had been melted and exported. The only way to arrest this influx of gold and efflux of silver was to readjust the ratio to that prevailing abroad; and both Locke and Newton seem to have recognised the advisability of achieving this object by altering the rating of the gold, without disturbing the value of the silver from that Elizabethan standard, which was regarded as fixed and unimpeachable by the monetary reformers of the reign of William the Third. But the action suggested by them was taken too late; and, owing to the new supplies of the yellow metal from Brazil, the value of gold compared with silver fell still further, and the overrated metal continued to displace the underrated silver, until at the time of the next recoinage, in 1774, the gold had become the preponderant metal in use, and to its deteriorated condition attention was now chiefly directed.

This last recoinage was effected at the suggestion of Lord Liverpool.[1] In consequence, apparently, of the quantity of light silver in circulation, and especially of silver coin of defective weight imported from abroad, silver was to be legal tender by tale only for less sums than twenty-five pounds, but it might still be legal tender by weight for any amount. This law expired in 1783, but was revived in 1798, and clauses were added, first suspending, and then prohibiting, the coinage of silver. At the resumption of cash payments the gold standard was formally introduced, the legal tender of silver was restricted to two pounds, and a heavy seigniorage was charged upon its coinage. These changes were in keeping with the tenor of Lord Liverpool's *Treatise*, and were carried out by his son as Prime Minister. But they seem in some respects to have gone beyond his real intentions. He suggested that the cost of coinage only (or, as it is technically termed, brassage) should be taken out of the silver, but the natural desire to defray the necessary expense of the resumption of cash payments by a larger seigniorage prevailed. Nor did he necessarily contemplate the impossibility of the mint being free to the coinage of token silver; but the Act of 1816 made this freedom dependent on a proclamation,

[1] *Cf.* "Silver Pound," chapter vii.

which was never issued, and it is doubtful whether the right of making it was, or was not, withdrawn by an act of 1870.

Such then is, in briefest outline, the monetary history of England during the last two centuries. In the account, which we have given, we have freely borrowed from Mr. Dana Horton's "Silver Pound," and it is impossible to read that book without being sensible of the mass of recondite learning on which it is founded, and of the probability of the conclusions, which the author has drawn from the study of original documents, even when they conflict with traditional opinion. In the subsequent chapters of the present inquiry we shall examine some of the more important consequences of the changes we have sketched. Those consequences did not disclose themselves until after an interval of time; and we have now only to investigate their immediate bearing on the period before us. We must be content with brief consideration. It must be remembered that at the time, when the free coinage of silver was suspended, the relation between the output of the metals was changing again, and gold was once more falling behind. It is therefore possible, or indeed probable, that the directions of the influx and efflux would have been reversed, and that the currency might have become preponderantly silver. The lack of silver coin, which undoubtedly was fraught with serious inconvenience during the progress of the war with France, might have been removed, or have been met by the introduction of a token coinage,[1] without

---

[1] This possibility seems to remove (*cf.* Mr. Barr Robertson in paper in *Statistical Journal* for September, 1895) much of the ground from

disturbance of the standard. When the suspension of specie payments was ended, the resumption might have been effected on a broader metallic basis, and the fall of prices, which continued to the fifties, not indeed prevented, but appreciably lessened. The inevitable ups and downs of credit would have been present, whether the currency were bimetallic, or monometallic on a silver basis; but the recovery from the periodic depression might have been less difficult and speedier to achieve, if the basis had been broader. A general fall there must apparently have been in any case; and, so far as the inconvertible bank-note had been issued to excess, suffering must have attended its contraction, just as it followed on the withdrawal at a later time of the excessive issues of the country banks. The question remains whether a broader metallic basis for the standard might have rendered the fall less severe and the suffering less acute.[1]

In the period under consideration it is impossible to disengage from the operation of other causes the influence of the fall of prices upon the general welfare. On the one hand there is no doubt that the period immediately previous, when prices were rising by leaps and by bounds, was one of extraordinary manufacturing and commercial progress, and that the close of the war, and the resumption of cash payments, were followed by serious and continued depression in trade and agriculture. On the other hand it is

the inferences drawn from the undoubted inconvenience of the older bimetallic currencies to the inadvisability of international bimetallism.

[1] *Cf.* Mr. Everett in evidence before Commission on Agriculture, qq. 18,796, etc.

equally indisputable that the condition of the wage-earner during the period of our early manufacturing development was the reverse of prosperous. But the other forces, which were in operation, were so tremendous that it is impossible—if, indeed, it is really possible in any case—to eliminate their influence and attribute the residuum to the action of money on prices. In the eighteenth, as in the sixteenth century, the break-up of the old order, and the substitution of the new, were remarkable and bewildering. Alike in their effects on the prosperity of the manufacturer and trader, and on the misery of the wage-earner and apprentice, on the permanent advance of the nation, and on temporary dislocation of social arrangements, the new inventions and the growth of the factory may be described as revolutionary. The great war, again, stands out among such conflicts for the magnitude of its cost and the importance of its results. Nor is it possible to say that the misery of the workman ended with the rise of prices,[1] or that the manufacturing development was arrested by the fall.

We cannot indeed expect to isolate the influence of changes in prices, and we must rather regard them as adding to, or taking away from, other influences. In the period, with which we are now dealing, those other influences are so remarkable that they seem to throw all else into the background. We are perforce driven back on probabilities; and from these we should infer that, while the sudden rise—for it was undoubtedly

---

[1] The reverse was certainly the case. *Cf.* Cunningham: "Growth of English Industry and Commerce," bk. viii., chaps. xxi., xxii. ; and also Spencer Walpole's "History of England" and Harriet Martineau's "History of the Peace.'

rapid from 1792 to 1809—was, like that in the sixteenth century, calculated on the one hand to dislocate industrial relations, and on the other to stimulate manufacturing enterprise, the steady fall, which followed, may have allowed time for the dislocation to be reduced, but must also have exerted some retarding influence on commercial progress. The consequences of the stimulus remained in an extended trade, while the evil effects on the condition of the labourer passed away, as his political standing improved, and his economic power increased. Both in the sixteenth century and in the period with which we are now dealing, the change from the old order to the new, which was due to causes different from any connected with the supplies of the precious metals, amounted to a revolution; and it is in quieter times that we are more easily able to trace in facts the confirmation or rebuttal of our theories. It is especially to the modern organisation of industry, inaugurated by the industrial revolution, where the function of the employer is conspicuous, and the system of credit elaborate, that those conclusions apply, at which we arrived, when in the second chapter we considered the possible effects of changes in prices on the economic condition of the general community. The period, that we are now approaching, partakes more fully of this character.

CHAPTER V.

THE RISE OF PRICES CONSEQUENT ON THE DISCOVERIES OF GOLD IN CALIFORNIA AND AUSTRALIA.

In the sixteenth century the supplies of the precious metals received an extraordinary addition from the mineral wealth of Mexico and Peru. For the space of three centuries the new silver found its way into the world in quantities, which, with some decline during the seventeenth from the high point reached at the beginning of that century, steadily increased during the eighteenth, and towards the close at an accelerated rate, until in the first decade of the nineteenth the volume of production attained an annual average of 894,150 kilograms according to Dr. Soetbeer's figures. During the earlier part of the eighteenth century the supplies of silver were supplemented in increasing force by Brazilian gold; but, with the disturbances in America at the close of the opening decade of the nineteenth century, the supplies of both metals underwent a sudden and serious decline. A steady fall in prices ensued, which, with the interval of a partial recovery in the fourth decade, due apparently to new gold from Siberia,[1] continued until the fresh discoveries of that metal in California in 1848, and in

[1] Which reinforced those Russian supplies from the Ural Mountains, which had begun to assume an important place in the previous decade.

Australia in 1851, furnished a parallel, by the magnitude and rapidity of their additions to the existing stock, to the memorable discoveries of three centuries earlier. Competent observers[1] ventured to predict that similar results would follow both with regard to prices and to the welfare of the community; and their predictions were proved untrue, not so much because they exaggerated the additions to the mineral wealth, as because they under-estimated the counteracting influences.

The world, in fact, into which the new gold came, was different from that existing at the discovery of America. The fresh supplies made their entrance with greater rapidity into the highways of commercial intercourse, and even penetrated with far less delay into many of the by-ways; and the stimulus naturally applied to the increase of production and population was more speedily manifest. Cairnes[2] has put forward as a partial explanation of the sufferings of the English labourer at the time of the influx of the new supplies from Spanish America the consideration that the prices of the goods, on which he spent his wages, rose in neutral markets before any corresponding advance in the prices of the goods that he produced; and, although it is true that the rise of prices was not uniform or universal in the nineteenth, it was likely to be less spasmodic than in the sixteenth century. There might, as Cliffe Leslie contended,[3] be districts, into which the Californian and Australian gold did

---

[1] Such as M. Chevalier in his "De la Baisse Probable de l'Or," which was translated into English by Cobden.
[2] "Essays in Political Economy," p. 150.
[3] *Ibid.*, xix., xx.

not penetrate. There were certainly countries and places, which came more tardily into contact with it, and were later in the upward movement of prices. There might be towns and trades, where the new supplies were introduced into a previous lower level of prices, and, when once they found an entrance, caused a more rapid and extensive advance than in those populous industrial centres where the previous level was higher. For reasons such as these the rise of prices consequent on the gold discoveries of the nineteenth century would so far resemble that of the sixteenth that it would proceed by a series of jerks. But the jerks were less extreme and less spasmodic. Trade was more evenly diffused. The channels of commercial intercourse were wider and deeper. The means of communication were easier and more effective; and, while local inequalities might prevail, they were less pronounced and less obstructive.

In short, the fall in the value of gold, to quote from Jevons' answer[1] to Chevalier and Cobden, who had anticipated a series of "innumerable shocks and sufferings," was "gradual and gentle." "Far from taking place with sudden and painful starts, flinging the rich headlong to a lower station, and shaking the groundwork of society, nothing," he remarked, "is more insidious, slow, and imperceptible." "It is insidious," he continued—in language which is full of instruction, and should be continually borne in mind in all inquiries into the nature and effects of changes in general prices—"because we are accustomed to use the standard as invariable, and to

---

[1] "Investigations," p. 78.

measure the changes of other things by it, and a rise in the price of any article, when observed, is naturally attributed to a hundred other causes than the true one. It is slow, because the total accumulations of gold in use are but little increased by the additions of any one or of several years. It is imperceptible because the slow rise of prices due to gold depreciation is disturbed by much more sudden and considerable but temporary fluctuations which are due to commercial causes and are by no means a novelty."

It was, then, into a world to which these remarks of Jevons were applicable, and not into the comparatively simple and primitive industrial and commercial economy of Elizabethan times, that the new gold from California and Australia made its entrance. That the discoveries were enormous is shown by statistics of their volume. The average annual production of gold in the second decade of the nineteenth century is stated by Dr. Soetbeer[1] to have amounted to 11,445 kilograms. By the fifth decade it had increased, largely in consequence of the output from Siberia, to 54,759 kilograms, and in this decade the Californian discoveries of 1848 had begun to take their place in the supply. These discoveries were followed in 1851 by those in Australia; and the annual production increased in the next five years to 199,388 kilograms. From that point it rose to a maximum of 201,750 kilograms in the five years extending from 1856 to 1860; and then a decline began.

Nor was the magnitude of the increase more remarkable than its suddenness. Between the fourth and the fifth decade of the century the annual pro-

[1] "Materialien," pt. i.

duction of gold exhibited an increase of 170 per cent., and in the next decade the increase amounted to about 290 per cent. In the following five years, when the highest point was attained, the increase on the production of a quarter of a century before was as much as 900 per cent. Such a large and rapid increase exceeded anything that had occurred in the sixteenth century, so far as Dr. Soetbeer's figures for that period show; nor are the statistics less remarkable when we turn from the volume to the value of the annual production.

In the fourth decade of the century the value of the annual production is estimated by Dr. Soetbeer at £2,830,300, in the fifth at £7,638,850, in the next five years at £27,815,400, and in the next five, when the highest point was reached, at £28,144,950. Thus the increase in a quarter of a century would appear to be about 1,300 per cent., and the value first more than doubled and then more than trebled itself. Although the production of silver advanced steadily, the percentage of the successive increase was comparatively small, and during part of the time, contrasted with the gold, might be deemed insignificant; and yet the total production of the two metals increased from £8,108,900 first to £14,506,500, then to £35,834,750, and, finally, to £36,380,400. In other words, it was more than quadrupled. The ratio of the total volume of the gold to that of the silver altered from 3·3 to 96·7 to 18·2 to 81·8, and the ratio of the value from 34·9 to 65·1 to 77·4 to 22·6.

Within the first decade that the United States became a considerable source of supply, the volume of production of the yellow metal increased in that country from 850 kilograms to 17,600,[1] and largely exceeded that furnished by any other country but Russia, where the annual yield amounted to 22,515 kilograms, and had increased to this figure from 7,050 kilograms in the previous decade. Of the total production for the whole world the United States, even in that decade, supplied somewhat less than a third. In the following five years the output increased to 88,800 kilograms, or, in other words, by a percentage of more than 400, and, together with the Australasian supply, which amounted to 69,573 kilograms, furnished 158,373 kilograms out of a total production of 199,388, or more than three quarters. Within a single year, according to the American statistics, the production of gold in that country increased from 889,085 dollars to 10,000,000, and in the subsequent year—that of 1849—there was a further increase to 40,000,000. In 1853 a maximum was reached of 65,000,000, or more than sixty-five times the production of the sixth year previous. In Australia the output of gold increased[2] from 357,019 ounces or 10,179 kilograms in 1851 to 3,105,286 ounces or 88,532 kilograms in 1852, and rose to a maximum of 3,292,150 ounces or 93,859 kilograms in 1853. The increase here amounted to between 800 and 900 per cent.

We may now proceed to inquire into the effect upon prices of this remarkable increase. In his pamphlet on "A Serious Fall in the Value of Gold,"[3] published

---

[1] Cf. Tables in *Statistical Journal* for June, 1894.

[2] According to Table prepared for the Report of the British Master of the Mint by the Master of the Melbourne Mint (given by Dr. Soetbeer in his "Materialien").

[3] Jevons' "Investigations," ii.

in 1863, fifteen years after the discoveries in California, and twelve after those in Australia, Jevons calculated the average fall in the purchasing-power of gold, measured by the change in the prices of 39 "chief" articles, between 1845-50 and 1860-62 at 14, and, measured by 64[1] "minor" articles, at 6·34 per cent. The total average fall he put at 9½ per cent., or the average rise of prices at 10¼ per cent. But the period, which he took as the terminus of this calculation, was, as he stated, one of "low water" in the commercial tide, and he anticipated that within half a dozen years later prices might rise to 40 or 50 per cent. above the average of the years from which he started. He pointed out that in 1857 the "prices at high tide were 29 per cent. above the average."

This prediction was not, however, fulfilled. In a subsequent letter to the *Economist*,[2] taking this time as his starting-point the year 1849—a year which, he observed, was specially adapted for such a purpose, because it was at once the first year of the gold discoveries and also the year in which prices reached the lowest point that, when he was writing, they had attained during the century—and, basing his calculations on the prices of about 50 articles, he found that the index number thus constructed showed a rise from 100 in 1849 to 101 in 1850, 103 in 1851, 101 again in 1852, and then made a sudden advance to 116 in 1853 and 130 in 1854, until in 1857 it had reached its maximum of 132. It then fell in 1858 to 118, and in 1860 was 124, in 1861, 123, and in 1862

---

[1] The original number taken was 79, but, by grouping, it was reduced to 64 "independent" articles.

[2] "Investigations," No. iv.

again 124, rising again in 1866 to 128, and falling to 119 in 1869, the year in which he was writing. Comparing the numbers for the three years of commercial collapse—1849, 1858, and 1867—when prices, so far as credit and its fluctuations were concerned, were presumably at their lowest point, he established a permanent rise of 18 per cent., which he considered to be due to the more deeply-seated cause of an alteration in the supplies of gold.

With the results thus attained by Jevons, whose inquiries into the subject may be treated as classical, we may contrast the conclusions shown by the index numbers of Mr. Sauerbeck [1] and of Dr. Soetbeer.[2] As we have noticed,[3] Mr. Sauerbeck employs a simple arithmetic mean, and starts with the average of the years 1867-77. His index number for 1849 is 74, and is the lowest for the whole century until that date. From 1849 the number increases until, in 1857—a period, no doubt, of speculative excitement—it reaches the figure 105. In 1864 also it was 105. The difference between the two years 1849 and 1857 is thus 31, while Jevons, taking 1849 as his *terminus a quo*, reached the number 132 in 1857. For the years 1860-2 Jevons estimated a rise of some 10 per cent. on the average of the years 1845-50 ; and, taking the single year 1849 as the starting-point of the calculation, the numbers for the three later years were 124, 123 and 124 again. Mr. Sauerbeck gives 74 for the earlier and 99, 98, and 101 for the later years, thus showing increases of 25, 24, and 27, against Jevons' 24, 23, and 24.

[1] *Cf.* paper in *Statistical Journal* for June, 1893.
[2] "Materialien," pt. vii.
[3] In the last chapter.

For the years 1858 and 1867, taking 1849 as the *terminus a quo*, Jevons' numbers are 118 in either case, and Mr. Sauerbeck's numbers are 91 and 100, being an increase of 17 for the former year, and of 26 for the latter, on the number for 1849. The general consilience of the results, when allowance is made for the difference in the numbers from which the calculations respectively commence, and the increases shown by Mr. Sauerbeck, are, like those of Jevons, reduced to percentages, is far more remarkable than the difference exhibited in the last case—that of the year 1867: and this is perhaps due to a cause indicated [1] by Jevons himself as responsible for the divergence between his own results and those of the *Economist*. In the index number of that newspaper 4 of the 22 articles, which formed the basis of the number, consisted of cotton, and the rise in the price of that commodity during the American Civil War, and the so-called "cotton famine," was nothing less than enormous. In Jevons' own number, starting with 1849, 3 of 50 commodities consisted of cotton, and a geometric mean, specially intended to correct undue influence, was substituted for the simple arithmetic mean of the *Economist*. In Mr. Sauerbeck's number it it true that only two places in 44 are assigned to cotton, but a simple arithmetic mean is taken, and, as he himself states,[2] "the extreme prices of cotton during the American Civil War" have "raised the general average considerably."

Turning to Dr. Soetbeer's number, which is based

---

[1] "Investigations," p. 154. The effect continued, of course, for some while after the war was ended.
[2] *Cf.* paper in *Statistical Journal* quoted above, p. 240.

on 114 commodities, (of which 100 are Hamburg and 14 English prices), and starts from the average of the years 1847-50, and adopts a principle, which in effect gives some amount of weighting to the general average,[1] we find that number is not given for 1849, but that in 1857 the rise is 30 per cent. on the average of 1847-50; in 1860-2 it is 20, 18, and 22; in 1858 it is 13; and in 1867 it is 24, as contrasted with advances of 32, 24, 23, 24, 18, and 18 shown by Jevons for the corresponding years. Mr. Sauerbeck's differences are 31, 25, 24, 27, 17, and 26; but in this case allowance must be made for the different number (74), from which the increase is reckoned. From a comparison of the three sets of numbers certain conclusions emerge. They agree in tending generally in one direction. That of Dr. Soetbeer resembles that of Mr. Sauerbeck in exhibiting a more marked advance in 1867 than that shown by Jevons, and this, as we have seen, is perhaps due to the influence exercised on the general average by the extraordinary rise in cotton. On the other hand Jevons is in accord with Mr. Sauerbeck in arriving at an advance, which, viewed throughout the series of years embraced, is greater than that indicated by Dr. Soetbeer. In appreciating the significance of this special difference, it should be remembered, as Mr. Sauerbeck urged before the Gold and Silver Commission,[2] that Dr. Soetbeer's number includes many

---

[1] By dividing the articles into groups, and giving an index number for each, and then working up to the final index number by treating the groups as equally important, although differing in the number of articles comprised. (*Cf.* Sir R. Giffen in evidence before Gold and Silver Commission, q. 753.)

[2] Q. 1,015, where he also argued that import prices (such as those on which Dr. Soetbeer's number is largely based) " follow movements

commodities, which may be described as "small," and, by comparison with those embraced in other numbers, such as Mr. Sauerbeck's own, considered unimportant. Mr. Sauerbeck himself, dealing with a later period, found that, by taking Dr. Soetbeer's figures for the same commodities only as his own, the difference between the two numbers was reduced; and at the time, with which we are now concerned, Jevons similarly discovered[1] that the inclusion of minor articles produced a noticeable diminution in the general average. On *a priori* grounds it would seem probable, both as respects a rise and as regards a fall, that the minor articles would be less responsive to the influence of changes in general prices, that they would not come so rapidly into contact with the supplies of the metals, and that the *vis inertiae* opposing an alteration would in their case be greater and more obstinate.[2] But the broad consilience of the results is more noticeable than the differences of detail; and of the fact of a marked and general rise of prices following on the gold discoveries of California and Australia little doubt can be seriously entertained.

The amount, however, of the rise, is noteworthy when contrasted with the evidence attainable of the occurrences of the sixteenth century. In its effects

---

more slowly than market prices," and that it is better to measure from high prices downwards than from low prices upwards. (*Cf.* also his paper in *Economic Journal* for June, 1895, and Mr. Pierson's reply in September, 1895.)

[1] *Cf.* "Investigations," No. ii.

[2] *Cf.* evidence of Sir R. Giffen before Gold and Silver Commission, q. 819, where he points out that the cost of manipulation and of distribution affect retail prices. (*Cf.* also below, chapter vi., on possible influence of wages on retail prices.)

on the welfare of the community, and on the relation of various classes to one another, an advance of 18 per cent., such as Jevons thought he had established in 1869, was not unimportant; but it sinks into insignificance when compared with the movement recorded at the earlier time. At that period Adam Smith, taking the price of corn alone, discovered a rise of some 200 per cent. in the seventy years between 1570 and 1640; and his conclusions have been substantially confirmed by those obtained by other means.[1] We may fittingly inquire into the explanation of this difference, which, whether we look at the effects on prices, or on the general welfare, places in distinct categories changes in the supplies of the metals in the modern world and similar alterations in Elizabethan times.[2] Such a difference dictates no small amount of caution in arguing from the experience of the earlier to the later age, and points to the likelihood that under the present industrial and commercial economy changes in the supplies of the metals will be more subtle and gradual in their operation, and more calculated to produce the effects—based partly on a real difference in the relation of debtor and creditor, and

---

[1] *Cf.* Newmarch's examination of the results reached by various inquirers, such as Arthur Young, in vol. vi., app. ii., of Tooke and Newmarch's "History of Prices," pp. 388, etc. The rise in France he puts at a similar figure, and dates its commencement from about 1570. Arthur Young's inquiry related chiefly to agricultural wages, but also to prices.

[2] Newmarch points out ("History of Prices") that even in the Elizabethan period a rise of 200 per cent. in prices was less than might, *a priori*, have been expected from the increase in the production of the metals, and that by 1640 the rise was apparently over, and the new silver only sufficed to meet the growth in demand caused by extended trade, etc.

partly on a sentimental influence exercised on the imagination — which were set forth in the second chapter of the present inquiry, when the question was examined of the balance of advantage and drawback between a rise and a fall. The sudden dislocation of the sixteenth century, aggravated, as it seems to have been, by the previous debasement of the coinage, is foreign to the conditions of the nineteenth, and the accompanying evils, and the specially injurious influence on the position of the wage-earner, are the less likely to be repeated.

At any rate, in the period, which we are now considering, no such sudden dislocation occurred, and no such rapid and excessive rise in prices was evident. It was anticipated, but it did not happen; and into some of the reasons we may now inquire. The first, most obvious, and most important, is found in the relative magnitude of the existing stocks of the metals. At the discovery of America these stocks were reduced to a very low sum; and Jacob puts the amount in coin at £33,000,000. This is a guess founded on more or less reliable data; and any corresponding estimate for the present day cannot pretend to more than conjecture. But it is not unlikely that the existing stock of coin in Europe at the time of the Californian and Australian discoveries may have been many times as great as it was three centuries earlier. The initial effect, therefore, of any increase in the annual additions was largely reduced; and the influence of the successive increments, which in any case would tend to diminish in consequence of the preceding, would decline at a more rapid rate in the nineteenth than in the sixteenth century. This diminution in the influence exerted by an increase in the annual output is distinguished [1] by Jevons as due to a " swelling" of the currency in contrast with what he terms an " extension "; and he believed that most of the writers on the probable effects of the new gold supplies had under-estimated the first of these forces and over-rated the second.

Yet that the currency would be " extended " by the growth of commerce and manufacture, stimulated, perhaps, by the new supplies of gold, but in any event naturally increasing with the progress of invention and the development of organisation, was inevitable. That this " extension " would exert a retarding influence on the advance of prices could not be questioned; nor could it be denied that such a cause was likely to operate with greater speed and intensity in the nineteenth than in the sixteenth century. Such an " extension " might take different forms, and among the more important would be a new expansive force given to credit.

The relation between the supplies of the metals and credit is a difficult problem; and the development of credit, with its substitutes for cash, is one of those incidents of the organisation of the modern world, which tends to obscure the connection between the metals and prices. How, it is sometimes asked,[2] do they come into contact? Prices in wholesale markets, to which index numbers relate, are generally determined without the passage of actual cash, and

---

[1] " Investigations," p. 69.

[2] *Cf.* Lord Farrer in " Gold, Credit and Prices." (*Cf.* also Lord Herschell in examination of witnesses before Gold and Silver Commission, qq. 9,640, etc.)

the transaction is effected by a credit-instrument—a cheque, it may be, or a bill of exchange. The multiplication of these instruments, it is contended, has resulted in a great economy of cash; and, as with the flow and ebb of credit they increase and decline, so prices rise and fall. The connection between the metals and prices is at the best indirect and remote, and is continually becoming more complex and obscure.

This argument is certainly right in denying the directness of the relation; but it seems no less true that a real connection exists between the metals and prices. The connecting link is discovered in the bank reserves.[1] In the last analysis, as Bagehot[2] and other inquirers have shown, the fabric of credit is found to be built on the cash-reserve in the Bank of England. Credit may indeed expand and contract. Its movements may be more extensive at one time than at another; but it rests on the reserves, and the connection is brought into prominence at times of commercial crises, when men turn with panic from credit to cash. Every banker in succession, from the Bank of England, the custodian of the ultimate cash-reserve, maintains, if he wishes to avoid insolvency, a proportion between his liabilities and his reserve. And thus the connection between the reserves, into which, in the modern banking world, the new supplies would naturally find their way at the outset, and credit, which, expanding and contracting of itself owing to alternations of speculative or stagnating

---

[1] *Cf.* Giffen: "Essays in Finance," second series, ii.: "Gold Supply: the Rate of Discount and Prices."
[2] In "Lombard St.," *passim*.

trade, is yet limited [1] in the extent of its movements by the basis of cash on which it is built, implies a real connection between the precious metals and prices. If the reserves increase, and promise to increase still further, a rise of prices, above the temporary advance due to a period of active speculation, will be produced; and, if the reserves diminish, and apprehension is felt of their further diminution, the fall, which would naturally follow contracting credit, will be accentuated. For this reason, to detect the deeper cause, which consists of changes in the supplies of the metals, we must eliminate the more superficial influence of credit-fluctuations. It may be that, with the increase of banking, a larger fabric of credit is habitually constructed on a narrower foundation of cash, and this "extension" of the currency may exert some counteracting influence to a diminution in the supplies of the metals. It is a circumstance to be noted when we are comparing over an interval of years the effects on prices of the precious metals; but it admits of some statistical verification, and, in the absence of evidence of important change, we may contrast the level of prices reached in one credit cycle with that attained in another, and conclude that, if the level be raised or lowered, the change is due, not to credit, but to some more fundamental alteration between the circumstances of the production of commodities and the supplies of the precious metals. Estimated by this test, there could be little doubt that at the period we are now examining the addition to the supplies of the precious metals had exerted an important influence on the course of general prices.

[1] *Cf.* Jevons' "Investigations," p. 32.

A further question, however, may be raised whether this development of credit, which admittedly renders the connection between the metals and prices less direct, increases or diminishes the influence of the one on the other. It might seem, on the one hand, as if the effects would be lessened as they are spread through a wider area; and yet, on the other, that their importance would be increased because so large a mass of business transactions is ultimately dependent on them.[1] Either view expresses apparently a portion of the truth. It would certainly seem that, considered simply with reference to immediate consequences, a relatively small change in the supplies of the precious metals, acting through the medium of so elastic and expansive an agency as credit, would produce a greater and wider effect on prices than would result if no such medium existed. But, on the other hand, it would also appear to be probable that the counteracting forces would be set in action more rapidly. The "extension" of trade would more speedily make its appearance, and what Jevons distinguished as the "swelling" of the currency consequent on depreciation would be sooner effected. The rise would be quickened, and, for the time, magnified; but the reaction, which it would tend to produce, would also be readier and more extensive. Regarding the matter thus, Cairnes reached the prediction,[2] verified by events, that the rise occasioned by the new gold from California and Australia would be more speedily completed in England, with its developed credit, than in

---

[1] *Cf* Professor Foxwell in *Economic Review* for July, 1893: "Bimetallism: Its Meaning and Aims," p. 316.
[2] "Essays in Political Economy," ii.

the less responsive and more absorbent currencies of the East, that the natural reaction would take place more rapidly with manufactured goods, which with ease and without delay could be produced in increasing quantities to meet an extended demand, and that the process would be tardier with raw materials, and that, amongst these, those of vegetable growth would answer more quickly to an increased demand than those of animal origin, which could only be produced after a longer interval.

Two further considerations must be borne in mind in estimating the total influence of credit. One is that it is a medium peculiarly sensitive, and probably serves to intensify the effects on the imagination of an increase or diminution in the supplies of the precious metals, and therefore accentuates also the consequent rise or fall of prices. The other consideration is more complex. If the general level of prices be raised, the smaller transactions of society, which are still conducted by cash, will require a larger quantity, and the demands on the banks for petty cash will become more urgent. This will occasion a drain on the reserves, into which the new supplies have come; and the volume of the currency will be increased, and the counteracting forces set in motion. It can hardly be doubted that the elevation of the general level of prices is effected with greater rapidity through the agency of credit; and therefore both the rise occasioned by the influx, and the reaction from the rise, seem likely to be accelerated by its presence.

In the relations thus established in the modern world between the precious metals and prices through the medium of credit and the reserves the explanation may be found of a paradox sometimes raised in such discussions.[1] When the new supplies find their way into the reserves, the bankers lower the rate of discount; for, with the enlargement of the basis of cash, they are in a position to extend the superstructure of credit. They are more able, and, unless they wish to keep the money idle, they are more ready, to increase their liabilities; and, therefore, they are willing to lend on more favourable terms—to discount merchants' bills at cheaper rates. The value of "money" is lower in the sense of loanable capital in the money market.

But this willingness to lend encourages traders to borrow and extend their business; and the increase of business leads in its turn to a rise of prices—to a fall in the value of "money," that is, in the sense of the measure of value. The rise of prices brings with it the advance of wages, and the demand for a larger quantity of petty cash; and now the bankers, in order to arrest the drain, are compelled to raise the rate of discount, unless a fresh or continued influx of the metals should furnish the means of meeting the growing demands. This elevation of the rate of discount will tend in its turn to check the extension of business and to arrest speculation. It will thus occasion a fall of prices and diminish the demand for petty cash for the payment of wages and for the purchase of retail goods. The tide will be reversed, and cash will flow back to the reserves instead of

[1] *Cf.* Mr. W. Fowler in evidence before the Gold and Silver Commission, qq. 7,705, etc.; and also Lord Farrer before the Commission on Agriculture, qq. 38,624, etc.

issuing out, and the bankers will reduce the rate of discount.

Thus changes in the rate admit of differing interpretations. The rate is an index at once of ability to lend and desire to borrow. It may be low, because sluggish trade, and falling prices, have occasioned less demand on the part of discouraged traders for loanable capital, and the tide moved by the need of cash for small payments has set towards instead of away from the reserves. Or it may be low, because bankers find that a continuous influx of the precious metals increases their ability to meet the growing demands for monetary accommodation, occasioned by brisk trade and rising prices. Or, once more, the rate may be high in consequence, either of the eagerness of this demand, or of the difficulty of replenishing the reserves. According to the circumstances of the moment, the variations of the rate may conceivably afford opposite indications of the state of trade and of general prices; and the value of money, in the sense of loanable capital in the money market, may differ from the value of money in the sense of the measure of value.

To these considerations, in any attempt to appraise the real significance of the rate of discount, and of changes, which are made in it, it should be added that the elevation of the rate is the agency employed by the Bank for attracting gold from abroad, and that loans are made for long periods of time as well as for those short periods, with which the rate is connected. An alteration in the rate may imply nothing more than a shifting in the "territorial distribution" of money, occasioned by a passing change in the balance of trade, and may not mean a permanent increase or diminution in the supplies from the mines, although it is true that it is by affecting the balance of trade that the new supplies make their way in succession into the different countries of the world. The permanent basis of credit, again, is to be found, not in the money available at any particular time in the money market, but in the capital existing in the country, and in the additions made thereto. A low rate of discount may imply a temporary abundance of the money in the money market, but may not mean a real growth of capital, or an addition to the permanent possibilities of the expansive force of credit. The rate is, in short, an index of the influx and efflux of bullion into and out of the country, into and out of the reserves. But a low rate may be a sign of stagnating trade as well as of ease in the money market, and may be found to co-exist with falling as well as with rising prices.[1]

Nor are large reserves a certain index of abundant supplies of the precious metals; for they may be hoarded against emergencies. They may, in fact, be the result of deliberate action, and not the natural consequence of economic forces. They may be due, not to abundance, but to a fear of scarcity. In modern times, and in civilised nations, the habits of hoarding have steadily yielded before the advantages of banking in the case of private individuals; and the accumulation of idle hoards by banks is not likely to be adopted as a continuous policy, if a favourable opportunity be presented for active employment of the money, and no special purpose for the hoard be enter-

[1] *Cf.* Prof. Marshall in evidence before Gold and Silver Commission, qq. 9,561, 9,678.

tained. But it is commonly believed that the rise of prices in the sixteenth century must have been arrested by extensive hoarding; and it is also thought, and attested by reliable authority, that during the troublous times of the Napoleonic Wars money was hoarded by individuals, and only brought into circulation at the conclusion of peace. Tooke, moreover, held [1] the view that any liberation of the metals from their use as money, effected by the issue of inconvertible paper during the Bank Restriction, was more than counteracted by the lavish expenditure of governments, not only on their armies in the field, but on hoards in their war-chests. This variety of hoarding is still extant in the Western world, and its influence on the values of gold and of silver is a factor, which cannot be neglected.

But the chief locality of hoarding by individuals is the East, and the absorbent character of Oriental currencies is ascribed in part to the prevalence of this disposition. It was, and to a great extent is still, true that the Indian, led by an instinct implanted by long experience of the ravages of succeeding conquerors, has contracted a habit of carrying a great portion of his accumulated wealth on his person in the form of adornment; and he contributes no inconsiderable quota to the consumption of the metals in the arts. It is also true that large quantities are hoarded in the East in the shape of coin or bullion.[2] At any rate, since the discovery of America, the East has exhibited a capacity for receiving and retaining

---

[1] *Cf.* "History of Prices," pt. iii., ch. ii., sec. 1.

[2] *Cf.* Sir D. Barbour in evidence before Gold and Silver Commission, qq. 1,090, etc.

the overflow of Europe, which has seemed illimitable.[1] Instead of passing the metal on to other countries, it has absorbed it in its currency; and the rise of prices, which, with the expansive force derived from credit, may be soon produced, and speedily completed, in Western nations, in the East occupies a longer period, and is at once more sluggish and more permanent.

Thus the drain to the East has been an influential factor in determining the effects of the supplies of the metals on prices since the Oriental trade became important; and, in comparing the rise, which formed the sequel of the conquest of Mexico and Peru, with that which followed on the Californian and Australian discoveries, we must remember that the Eastern trade was much larger in the nineteenth than in the sixteenth century. In the interval gold had indeed come from Asia into Europe, and about 1832 the tide, as we saw in the preceding chapter, had been actually reversed, and for a time there was a balance of export over import of treasure in the Indian trade. But for the years 1810 to 1813 Dr. Soetbeer[2] puts the annual imports into the three Indian Presidencies at forty million marks, or two million pounds. After the abolition of the monopoly of the East India Company he estimates them at more than twice that amount. From 1834 to 1850 he places the annual net import at two and a half millions; but in 1851 to 1855 the excess of import doubled that of the previous

---

[1] Sir D. Barbour ("Theory of Bimetallism," chapter xx.) suggests that such an illimitable capacity of absorption cannot be safely postulated in the future.

[2] "Materialien," pt. iii., 3.

quinquennium, and in that which succeeded it more than quadrupled the figures of the later period. With some variations, this high level was maintained during the following decade.

This large increase in the balance of import over export was partly due to the natural growth of the Eastern trade, but it was specially influenced [1] by the payments required on account of the suppression of the Mutiny, and of the deficiency in the American cotton crop during the Civil War, and its replacement by Indian cotton. The point, however, which calls for particular attention in connection with the gold supplies, is that by far the larger proportion of the treasure, which thus entered India, was not the fresh gold, which was pouring out of the new mines, but was, on the contrary, silver.[2] It might therefore have seemed as if the drain to the East would exert no arresting influence on the fall in the value of gold. The connecting link was furnished by the French bi-metallic mint. That mint received the gold, and released the silver, which thus found its way to the East. The broad evidence of the figures is unmistakable. The net imports of gold into France apparently increased [3] from a negative quantity in 1847 to 38 million francs in 1848, to 85 millions in 1851, to 289 millions in 1853, to 416 millions in the following year, and to a maximum of 539 millions in 1859. With the exception of one or two years [4] there seems to have been a balance

---

[1] *Cf.* Barbour: "Theory of Bimetallism," ch. xx.

[2] Gold was also imported in increased quantities in the years following the discoveries in California and Australia.

[3] *Cf.* Shaw: "History of Currency," p. 183.

[4] Mr. Barr Robertson, in paper quoted below, gives the years 1860 and 1861.

of import over export—varying, indeed, but generally very considerable—from 1848 to 1870. Before that time the balance had for several years inclined the other way by comparatively slight amounts. With regard to silver the position was apparently reversed.[1] From 1822 to 1851 the imports had exceeded the exports, but from 1852 to 1864 the balance inclined decidedly in the other direction. The statistics of coinage tell the same tale;[2] and from this "ostensive instance," as it may be called in Baconian language, the operation of the bimetallic system is clearly demonstrated. If ever a theory was verified by fact it was in this case.

Nor can it be doubted that this absorption of the gold, and release of the silver, exercised a controlling influence on their relative values. We have already noticed[3] that in the period subsequent to the discovery of America a remarkable change was evident both in the total volume and in the total value of the annual production of the two metals respectively, and yet the attendant change in their market ratio was comparatively inconsiderable. Although, with the increasing output of silver, the ratio steadily became more favourable to gold, an alteration from 1 to 10 to 1 to 15½ was not commensurate with what might have been fairly expected to follow on a change in the proportion of the total volume of production from 11 to 89 to 1 to 98, or in the total value from 57 to 43 to 23 to 76. It is impossible not to ascribe some steadying influence to the

---

[1] *Cf.* Shaw, "History of Currency," p. 184.
[2] *Ibid.*, *cf.* also Soetbeer: "Materialien," pt. iii., and J. Barr Robertson's paper in *Statistical Journal* for September, 1895.
[3] Chapter iii.

large use of silver in the currencies of the world; and it is at least noteworthy that the advance in the relative value of gold to silver was not diffused evenly over the whole period, but occurred by what Dr. Soetbeer terms[1] a "quick and sudden" change between 1621 and 1650. From this he draws the natural inference that the change could not be attributed to the conditions of production, although he allows that the effects of the new discoveries of silver might have been postponed for a time. The continuous wars, and the growth of international trade, occasioning increased demands for gold, are believed by him to be the causes most largely responsible. It is not, however, the rise before 1660, which so much concerns us now, as the comparative steadiness[2] since that date; and such an experience certainly seems to point to the conclusion that to deny a steadying influence to a bimetallic system, is not merely to contest the theory of supply and demand, but to reject the testimony of obvious facts.

In 1666 the principle of free and gratuitous coinage was adopted in England, and, with a temporary suspension of the coinage of gold at the time of the recoinage under William the Third, and the more permanent suspension of the coinage of silver in 1798, the English mint was open to both metals during the intervening hundred and thirty years. It is true that some obstruction to mintage in general appears to have been offered in practice by the authorities of the Bank during the years immediately preceding the later and

---

[1] "Materialien," ii.
[2] The "noteworthy stability," as Dr. Soetbeer calls it.

permanent restriction.[1] But from 1803 to the suspension, some twenty years ago, of the free coinage of silver at the mints of the Latin Union, the Paris mint was similarly open to the unlimited coinage of both metals, at a fixed ratio, and from 1865 the mints of Belgium, Italy, Greece and Switzerland were also open. During this period the production of the metals underwent very considerable change.[2] For the first decade of the nineteenth century the volume of gold was to silver as 1·9 to 98·1, in the fifth decade it became 6·6 to 93·4, with the first half of the sixth the influx of the new supplies from California and Australia altered it to 18·4 to 81·6. In the three succeeding quinquennia it was 18·2 to 81·8, 14·4 to 85·6, 12·7 to 87·3, and in 1871-5 it became 8·1 to 91·9. The alterations in the respective proportions of the total values were equally remarkable. Starting with 23·7 to 76·3, the relation became successively 24·7 to 75·3, 32·7 to 67·3, 34·9 to 65·1, 52·7 to 47·3, 77·6 to 22·4, 77·4 to 22·6, 72·1 to 27·9, 69·4 to 30·6, and 58·5 to 41·5. And yet, as the Gold and Silver Commissioners stated in their final report,[3] the ratio did not diverge more than three per cent. in either direction from the middle of the seventeenth century until 1873, while—to quote again their authoritative opinion—it had not "materially varied from $15\frac{1}{2}$ to 1" since the commencement of the present century. This comparative steadiness, coupled with the change produced after the suspension of the free

---

[1] *Cf.* Prof. Foxwell in evidence before the Commission on Agriculture, q. 22,823.
[2] Soetbeer: "Materialien," i.
[3] Sec. 7.

coinage of silver at the mints of the Latin Union some twenty years ago, is a noteworthy fact. Taken in conjunction with the theory of the compensatory action [1] of the bimetallic system, which, as students of Economics are aware, is an application to the sphere of money of a recognised extension of the theory of supply and demand, it surely constitutes that experimental verification of theory by fact, which is so difficult to discover in the region of the moral as contrasted with the physical sciences.

It is true that even here an argument based on the plurality of causes has been employed, and we are told on high authority [2] that, had not the circumstances favoured, the result would not have followed, and therefore the result is due, not to the action of the bimetallic system, but to the favouring circumstances. Such an argument may be admitted as a conceivable explanation of the stability of the ratio during the time when the bimetallic system was in operation; but its adequacy is not increased by a consideration of the events, which have followed the suspension of the system. The position seems to present itself thus. The presence of the system, in spite of great changes in the respective volume of production of the two metals, was accompanied by remarkable stability in their ratio.[3] The removal of the system, although the changes in the respective volume of produc-

---

[1] Cf. Jevons: "Money and the Mechanism of Exchange," ch. xii.
[2] Cf. Giffen: "Case against Bimetallism," ii., vi.
[3] Mr. J. Barr Robertson, in the paper quoted above, argues that the market price would always differ slightly from the mint price, if the bullion dealers were to get a profit, and the movement of bullion was to continue.

tion have not been more considerable or revolutionary than those, which occurred during its existence, has been attended by great instability in the ratio. If this is not as convincing an application of the combined methods of agreement and difference as we are likely to encounter in economic experience, it would, at least, be hard to discover a parallel. That the bimetallic system exercised a steadying influence on the relative value of the precious metals, and helped to arrest the fall of gold after the discoveries in California and Australia, rests on as logical a foundation as can well be found for any like assertion. The conclusion remains valid, whatever may be felt about the influence of other contributory causes in the past, whatever opinion may be held on the possibility of forming or maintaining in the future an union of nations sufficiently strong to counteract, by the demand for coinage at their mints, such changes in supply as are likely or conceivable, and whatever dispute be raised on the precise meaning to be attached to the agio or premium found on the one, or other, or on both, of the metals at different times in bimetallic France.[1] Some of these questions turn on points of fact, and some on considerations of theory; but they do not upset the reasoning, which recognises in the bimetallic system an arresting influence to the fall in the value of gold, and the divergence in its relation to silver, which, in the absence of the system, might

[1] *Cf.* Giffen: "Case against Bimetallism," pp. 58, etc ; Gibbs: "Colloquy on Currency," (3rd edition), Tables on pp. 24, 103-7; Prof. Foxwell in evidence before Commission on Agriculture, q. 24,179 ; Mr. J. Barr Robertson in paper in *Statistical Journal* for September, 1895, vol. lviii., pt. iii., especially pp. 427, etc.

have been expected to follow on the discoveries in California and Australia. The importance of this discussion and conclusion will be more evident in the next and final stage of the inquiry, with which we shall be occupied in the following chapter.

Of the effects of the rise of prices on the general welfare of the community it is unnecessary to treat at any length. The period was admittedly an epoch of great economic progress; and the gold discoveries are generally allowed to have been one of the contributory causes,[1] among which the introduction of free trade[2] and the construction of railways[3] were conspicuous. In every period the influence of variations in the supplies of the metals is properly regarded, not as nullifying or superseding the operation of other causes, but as supplementing or modifying their effects. Such a conception does not imply that the variations themselves are unimportant, but that they are less obtrusive, and less readily recognised. In estimating the effects of the changes at the period, which we are discussing, it should be remembered that the industrial and commercial economy of England was now so constituted that the good might be produced without the evil. The rise of prices was comparatively gentle, and so imperceptible to the ordinary observer that it was long before the true cause was commonly acknowledged. The evidence, which is available, seems to show that wages did not, as in the sixteenth century, follow the rise of prices at a distant, but at a

---

[1] Newmarch ("History of Prices," vol. vi., pt. vii., sec. 1, p. 135) considers them the most important.
[2] *Ibid.*, vol. v., pt. iv.   [3] *Ibid.*, pt. iii.

short interval.¹ There was no sudden dislocation of mutual relations, while there was undoubtedly a powerful incentive to business enterprise.

The tendency of the economic movement was inclining in favour of the workman; and it is probable that a real change of distribution was in process. In any case it seems likely that his real position would have advanced apart from any increase in its monetary expression. To effect the readjustment to this altered expression might require disputes, and engender irritation, just as the real change itself might not be accomplished without friction. This friction would undoubtedly be a hindrance to production; but, on a general view of the circumstances, and of the considerations advanced in the second chapter of the present inquiry, it is not improbable that the two movements may have helped rather than proved an obstacle to one another. The employer would undoubtedly be encouraged by the rise of prices, and, with brisker trade, would be more disposed to grant concessions to his workmen, while they would feel a greater consciousness of the improvement in their condition than they would have been likely to entertain, if their wages had remained stationary, and prices had fallen. At any rate, there do not seem to be any serious grounds for thinking that the wage-earning classes did not share in the benefit of the stimulus applied to business by the gold discoveries

---

¹ There is some reason for thinking that the direction of the movement shown in the sixteenth may have been reversed in the nineteenth century, and that the wages of those engaged in producing manufactured goods rose before the price of the food on which they spent their wages.

of the middle of the century, or that the advance in their position, which was probably proceeding before and continued after, was interrupted. Indeed, it seems rather to have been manifestly accelerated.

Nor can it be questioned that the burden of debt was sensibly reduced; and in the nineteenth century, national indebtedness, like the obligations of individual traders, working with borrowed money, had become an important factor in the social and industrial economy. It was true, and must be freely admitted, that widow and orphan might suffer; but it was also true, and served as a counterweight, that living active energy was benefited at the expense of inactive inherited accumulation. That a stimulus was given to the forces, which were making for increased production, which accelerated their pace, and extended the sphere of their operation, seems as unquestionable as that no serious or lasting injury was inflicted on the wage-earner, and no suffering on creditors, which could be regarded as outweighing, or even as equivalent to, the general benefits conferred. Such at least is the deliberate judgment of sober and competent inquirers, like Jevons[1] and Newmarch;[2] and the judgment does not conflict, but accords, with *a priori* theory and with attested fact.

[1] In passage quoted above, page 140, from "Investigations."
[2] "History of Prices," vol. vi., pp. 135, 192, 193, 216, etc., 235, 236.

CHAPTER VI.

THE FALL OF PRICES DURING THE LAST TWENTY YEARS.

We have now reached the final stage of our inquiry; and, before we address ourselves to its consideration, we may briefly review the conclusions reached in the preceding chapters. We shall thus obtain a more accurate conception of the kind of results that we may reasonably expect to secure. That the precious metals exert an influence on prices in the modern commercial world, which is not unreal because it is indirect; that the movement thus occasioned is only discernible over an interval of time, and must be distinguished from the more frequent and obvious fluctuations of credit; that the distinction can be effected by comparing the level of one credit cycle with that of another; that a change in prices consequent on an alteration in the supplies of the precious metals is not likely to be immediate, or uniform, or universal; that it will probably set in operation counteracting causes, which will serve at once to mitigate and to conceal its effects; that the influence of changes in prices on the welfare of the community, and of particular classes, must be regarded as supplementing, rather than superseding, the action of other causes; that the beneficial consequences of a rise, and the depressing influences of a fall, are more apparent and operative in modern industrial and commercial society, where the functions of the employer as the initiating and directing agent in trading and manufacturing enterprise receive a new prominence, and the presence and action of credit, with its sensitiveness to real or sentimental motives, and its opportunities for the play of the imagination, are more prevalent—all these considerations have been suggested by the investigations of the previous chapters, and they will apply to the examination on which we are now entering, when we approach the period embraced by the last twenty years.

The fall in prices during that period is attested by various index numbers. The general agreement of the results, in spite of differences of detail in the construction of the numbers, and of the precise degree of fall indicated, is remarkable, and is adequate to establish the fact of a noteworthy change. Mr. Sauerbeck's number may be taken as a type. That has fallen from a maximum of 111 in 1873 to 68 in 1893, and 63 in 1894.[1] It is true that the first year was one of unusual business activity consequent on the outburst of trade, which followed the Franco-German War. But the number 68 was lower than any point in the century anterior to the discoveries in California and Australia, and had never been reached before the year 1887. The number 63 was quite unprecedented. The general inclination of the curve of prices since 1873 has been steadily downwards, with brief upward oscillations at periods of expanding

[1] *Cf. Statistical Journal* for March, 1895, vol. lviii., pt. i., pp. 140, 154. During the last year (1895) the number tended to rise according to Mr. Sauerbeck's monthly statement, but the annual average was still as low as 62.

credit. After the gold discoveries the level reached at the highest point of each succeeding credit cycle was higher, and the lowest point attained in each depression, which followed on the speculative activity, was higher also. Since 1873 the position has been reversed. After each recovery the curve of prices has sunk lower, and each succeeding recovery has failed to rise to the level of its predecessor. By this failure to recover the old position, and this tendency to fall to a lower level, the underlying forces of the precious metals manifest their influence on the more superficial fluctuations of credit. They do not supersede those fluctuations, but accentuate or modify them; and credit-influences no more set them aside than they nullify the operation of credit.

The full significance, however, of the figures, which we have quoted, can only be appreciated in the light of Mr. Sauerbeck's additional comparisons. The number 63 was, he observes, "37 per cent. below the standard period" (which is the average of the decade 1867-77), "20 per cent. below the ten years 1878-87, and 9 per cent. below the average of the last ten years." Taking decennial periods, again, as the basis for a more general average, the average for the decade 1874-83 was 90, and for the decade 1884-93 was 71. In the decade 1848-57 it amounted to 89, and in the succeeding decade to 99. Here, again, the most recent decade was the lowest of the century. These results are in general accord with those attained by other index numbers. It is true that, so far as it has gone, Dr. Soetbeer's number has shown a less extensive fall; but the difference seems to be due partly to the particular point from which the calculation starts, and partly to the fact that it includes a great number of commodities of minor importance; and, though the fall indicated may be less in amount, the general direction of the movement of prices is similar. About the fact of a considerable decline since 1873 no serious question can be entertained, so far as the index numbers are reliable.

But it has been contended that they fail to afford certain testimony of changes in general prices. Their sufficiency is questioned, partly on the ground of defects of construction, and partly of the alleged inadequacy of the basis on which they are built. Of defects of construction no more need be said than that in recent years index numbers have undergone the most careful scientific testing, with the significant consequence, that attention to certain ideal requirements has not been found to produce any commensurate or material effect on the general result.[1] Although differing in detail of construction, all the well-known varieties furnish results, which are generally similar. They rest, however, on a similar basis; and, therefore, if there be a fault in the foundation, its unimportance would not be proved by similarity in the results reached by examining the superstructure. The fault would be common, and would issue in similar consequences.

From a dearth of reliable statistical material, index numbers consist of wholesale prices, and, for the most part, of those of unmanufactured goods; and, it is urged, that to obtain a true measure of changes in

---

[1] *Cf.* Reports of the Committee of the British Association quoted in chapter i., and Sir R. Giffen in paper in *Statistical Journal* for December, 1888, pp. 722, 723.

the general purchasing-power of money, retail prices, the prices of manufactured goods, and the prices of services or wages should also be included.[1] The absence of reliable data is, in the last analysis, the final answer to this contention in the case of the first two sets of prices. But it is also highly probable that, when a number embraces such important articles as those employed by Mr. Sauerbeck, it may be taken as fairly representative of the mass of commodities, and that the prices, both of manufactured goods, and of retail transactions, move in general sympathy with those of wholesale dealings, and of raw materials. In support of such a probability a considerable body of experience can be brought forward, and the onus of proof may surely be said to lie on the other side.[2] It is true that greater friction prevails in the retail than in the wholesale market, and that the *vis inertiæ* of custom delays inevitable change. But it is very improbable that the movement of retail prices should be in the opposite direction to that of wholesale; and, therefore, although the measure of the general change, as indicated by the index number, may be exaggerated, the direction can hardly fail to be correct. With regard to manufactured articles the same general considerations apply; but, as the broad tendency of advancing civilisation seems to be to diminish the cost of manufacture compared with the cost of obtaining the raw material, it is probable that, when prices are falling, an index number based on raw materials

---

[1] *Cf.* Lord Farrer in evidence before Commission on Agriculture, qq. 32,280, etc.
[2] *Cf.* Sir R. Giffen in paper quoted above.

may underrate the fall, as, when they are rising, it may exaggerate the rise.

The opposite would seem to be the case with wages. It is an attested fact of economic experience that, like retail prices, they are slow to change, and they do not alter so rapidly as prices generally. On the other hand, they differ from manufactured goods, and, we may add, from retail prices, which relate also to manufactured goods, because the broad tendency of progress in the modern world inclines to an alteration in the distribution of wealth in favour of the workmen, and to an advance in wages. When prices, therefore, are rising, the inclusion of wages in an index number would probably increase the rise, and, when they are falling, it would tend to diminish the fall. A real change in distribution may thus obscure the natural effects of changes in prices. Wages may remain stationary, though the purchasing-power of money has increased, because a change is simultaneously affecting the share of wealth falling to the workman. For this reason a combination of wages or incomes generally with the prices of commodities in an index number tends to beget confusion; and it seems to be more conducive to a clear appreciation of the movement of economic forces to make distinct inquiries into incomes and into prices.

It may be added that a regard for the importance of the employer as the initiator and director of industry would tend to increase the weight to be attached to the prices of wholesale commodities, and to prices generally, as distinct from wages; but such considerations may seem more apposite, when we take into account the cause, to which the change in the relative value of money and commodities during the last twenty years is due.

On this question an eager debate has been conducted. Does the cause, it is asked, lie primarily with the commodities or with the money? As we saw, in the first chapter, a mere inspection of the index number will only eliminate the influence of different minor causes, acting on various commodities in opposite ways, and of temporary causes, the effects of which are transitory. Particular accidents of supply and demand will disappear in the general average, unless the change be very marked. This was the case with cotton during the American war; but in such instances the compensating circumstance is present that the disturbing influence is so considerable that it cannot escape detection. It will attract notice, and express allowance can be made, without impairing the validity of the general conclusion. By taking a wide survey of time, as well as of commodities, the more transitory, and recurrent, fluctuations of credit can also be eliminated. But, if some common cause be affecting commodities, its influence will not be removed, or neutralised, by any enlargement of the number of articles, on which the calculation rests. It will appear, and must be recognised, in the general average. On the other hand, by extending the time covered by the survey, it is often possible to determine whether such a common cause is a complete or sufficient explanation of the facts. If it was present, when the course of prices was tending in the opposite direction, we are forced to conclude that some new cause has been needed to produce the change.

It is very commonly asserted that the fall in prices

of the last twenty years is due to improvements in production and transportation;[1] and it cannot be denied that the natural effect of such a cause would be an increase in commodities, and a change in their relation to money, if there were no corresponding improvement in the production of the precious metals themselves. But this process of improvement is a cause, which has been continually in operation, and did not commence with 1873. The question, to use the instructive comparison of Sir Robert Giffen,[2] must be conceived "dynamically" and not "statically." As Jevons argued[3] on the fall of prices during the first part of the present century, when a similar cause was assigned, the same cause was operating previously when prices were rising, and, therefore, the change, which occurred, when prices, instead of continuing to rise, began to fall, must have been due to some different cause. Taking a general survey of the movement of prices during the century, we find that improvements in production have progressed throughout, but that prices rose at first, and then fell, until, with the gold discoveries of California and Australia, they rose again, again to fall after 1873. The movement of improvements in production sets steadily in one direction, while the movement of prices inclines first upwards, and then downwards, and then up, and down again. The only ground, on which these opposite changes could be attributed solely to one and

---

[1] *Cf.* Lord Farrer in evidence quoted above before the Commission on Agriculture, and Mr. W. Fowler in evidence before the Gold and Silver Commission.

[2] In paper quoted above, p. 173.

[3] "Investigations," pp. 110, 132.

the same cause—that of improvements in production—would be a reversal of this movement of improvement during the periods when the direction of the curve was changed. The argument that the movement of improvement in production proceeded at an accelerated speed during the periods of falling, and at a slackened rate in those of rising prices, is insufficient; for a positive reversal, and not a mere variation in relative rapidity, of the movement of prices is the fact to be explained. It may be allowed that part of the fall since 1873 is due to improvements in production. It may even be admitted—although the evidence seems to be by no means conclusive—that those improvements have proceeded with accelerated speed. But, when ample recognition has been given to these considerations, the phenomena of prices are not explained. Some other cause must still be sought. Some part at least of the fall must be due to the absence of a cause in operation when the rise was manifested, or to the presence of some cause, which then was absent.

Such a conclusion is reached by inspection of the index number, and by consideration of the adequacy of the cause alleged. We are led to seek for some other cause; and, if we can discover one, which can be shown to have been in operation, and to be competent to produce the effect, the probability that it is the cause, for which we are seeking, is so great as to amount to practical certainty.

The cause is to be found, not so much in the altered circumstances of the production of the precious metals as in the changes of demand. Or, perhaps, it would be more accurate to say that the cause must be sought in the combined action of the two factors. That an alteration in the respective volume of production of gold and silver occurred coincidently with a change in the respective demand for them as standard money measuring prices is a complete statement of the case. The production of gold had, until the last few years, declined from the level reached at the time of the Californian and Australian discoveries; and figures quoted[1] by the Gold and Silver Commission from Dr. Soetbeer show that the average annual supply in kilograms during the five years ending with 1885 was about 25 per cent. below the production of the years 1856-60. The estimated annual value for the later period was 20 millions, and for the earlier 28. Since the Commission reported the production has increased; and the present prospects, and realised results, of the new gold fields of Southern Africa and Western Australia point in the direction of a further, perhaps considerable, increase. Sir Robert Giffen, in evidence given in 1894 before the Commission on Agriculture, quoting the figures of the Director of the United States Mint, stated[2] that the production had again reached the 28 millions, which was the high-water mark of the discoveries in California and Australia. More recent statistics[3] establish a further advance to some 36 millions.

The production of silver, on the other hand, steadily increased throughout the period under review. The Gold and Silver Commissioners, again quoting from Dr. Soet-

---

[1] *Cf.* Final report, sec. 33.
[2] Q. 18,195.
[3] Report of Director of United States Mint issued in June, 1895, for 1894.

beer, found[1] that the annual production in kilograms for the quinquennial period ending with 1885 was 2,861,709 as compared with an annual production of 904,990 kilograms in 1856-60. The estimated value, converting the volume at the ratio of the day, which had already sunk from 15½ to 1 to 18·6 to 1, was more than two and a half times as great at the later as at the earlier period. Since then the volume of production has increased by more than two-thirds, and become some five or six times as great as it was in 1856-60.[2]

Such are the chief features of the changes in the volume of production. While in the period of the gold discoveries of the middle of the century the proportion of gold to silver in the total production had risen as high as 18·4 to 81·6, by the time of the Gold and Silver Commission it had sunk again to 5 to 95. In the case of the total values from 77·4 to 22·6 it had fallen to 49·3 to 50·7; and it has since fallen to a yet lower level. At the time, however, of the gold discoveries, changes in the volume of production occurred in the opposite direction of as great a magnitude; and yet, according to the authoritative statement of the Gold and Silver Commission, the effect on the ratio was scarcely perceptible throughout the whole course of the century up to 1873. Since then the alteration has been astonishing, and the ratio has advanced in favour of gold until it has become as much as 1 to 34. At the time of the Gold and Silver Commission it was 1 to 18·63. In the light of phenomena like these the conclusion that

[1] Report, sec. 12: "Materialien," pt. i.
[2] Cf. appendix xii. to vol. iii. of evidence before Commission on Agriculture.

the rupture of the bimetallic tie in 1873, by the suspension of the free coinage of silver at the mints of the Latin Union, must have exercised some influence in causing the divergence, would appear to be inevitable; and to such a conclusion accordingly the Gold and Silver Commissioners gave their unanimous assent.[1]

In the present inquiry we are not concerned so much with the immediate and admitted consequences of the suspension of the free coinage of silver in dislocating the par of exchange, as with its ulterior effects, combined with those of other monetary changes, upon the movement of gold prices. The bimetallic system had exerted a steadying influence on the market ratio between gold and silver—so important that, with opposite changes of revolutionary extent in the volume of production, the divergence in the ratio had been hardly perceptible. With the removal of this controlling influence the ordinary market forces were allowed free play, and the value of gold measured in silver rose. This change necessitated, if the real relation was to be preserved, some readjustment between silver prices in countries, where silver was the standard, and gold prices, where that metal was the standard, so far as they were engaged in commercial intercourse with one another. Such was the position of India and England; and it was inevitable that either silver prices should rise in India or gold prices fall in England. Some expectations were entertained[2] that the adjustment would be effected by the former process; but there were a

[1] Secs. 189, 192, 194.
[2] *Cf.* Bagehot on the "Depreciation of Silver."

priori reasons for thinking this unlikely, and the evidence of actual experience has confirmed these reasons.[1] Prices in an Oriental country, where custom is powerful, and the spirit of business enterprise inelastic, are rigid, when compared with the rapid movement and constant stir of the industrial and commercial economy of Western Europe. If, therefore, a readjustment in relative prices becomes inevitable, it is more likely to be effected in the country, where the *vis inertiæ* resisting change is weaker. The dislocation, accordingly, of the relations of exchange, implied in the removal of the steadying influence of the bimetallic system, involved some readjustment of prices between gold and silver-using countries in articles, which formed the subject of their commercial intercourse; and, where the countries in question were the slowly changing East and the restless West, the readjustment was likely to be effected in the latter rather than the former. This *a priori* probability has been confirmed by actual experience. Until recently, prices in India, which were silver prices, had not risen;[2] and prices in England, which were gold prices, had fallen. We have dwelt on this circumstance, because it affords some indication of the manner in which, with all that modern extensive development of credit, and that apparent indirectness of the connection between the precious metals and prices, which came under our notice in the

---

[1] *Cf.* Prof. Nicholson on "Money and Monetary Problems." Essay on the "Causes of Movements in General Prices." (*Cf.* also his article in *Economic Journal* for March, 1894, vol. iv., No. 13.)

[2] *Cf.* Gold and Silver Commission Report, sec. 52; Sir R. Giffen in paper in *Statistical Journal* for December, 1888; Commission on Agriculture, q. 23,694.

last chapter, it is possible for changes in the value of the metals in countries, like those of the East, where the currency is preponderantly metallic, and the metals are in direct contact with prices, to exercise some influence on the course of prices in the case of articles, which are the subject of commercial intercourse, in the more elaborately organised business communities of the Western world.

The removal, then, of the steadying influence of the bimetallic system was likely to occasion some alteration in gold prices; for it occupied a place in a series of monetary changes, which tended to throw a greater strain on the resources of the gold supplies. The full importance of these changes can only be appreciated by remembering that they began to operate, when the production of gold was declining, and had fallen some 25 per cent. below the high-water mark of the Californian and Australian discoveries. If the supply of an article diminishes, while the demand for it increases, a rise in its value is inevitable; and that after 1873 a decline occurred in the annual supply of gold, accompanied by a series of extraordinary additions to the demand, rests on the evidence of well-attested facts.

Before the Gold and Silver Commission in 1886 Sir Robert Giffen estimated [1] these extraordinary additions at some 200 millions. They consisted of 80 millions obtained by Germany between 1871 and 1875 for the adoption of a gold standard, and the execution of a simultaneous banking reform, extinguishing notes of small denominations, of 100

[1] Qq. 489, etc. (Cf. also his "Essays in Finance," first series, xiv.; second series, i., ii.)

millions taken by the United States on the resumption of specie payments in 1875 and the following years, and of 16 millions raised by loan for the resumption of specie payments in Italy. In evidence given some eight years later before the Commission on Agriculture, in 1894, Sir Robert Giffen stated [1] that the Italian demand had proved unreal, but that in the interval an additional extraordinary demand of perhaps 30 or 40 millions had been made by the Austro-Hungarian Empire,[2] which was preparing to resume specie payments on a gold basis, and of some 70 millions by Russia for the purpose of a military war-chest. Such a large extraordinary demand as 190 or 200 millions, coming upon an annual addition to the existing stocks of some 20 millions, could scarcely be met without exerting an influence on the value of the metal. And, even with the later increased annual production, such a demand as 30 or 40 or 70 millions could hardly fail to produce an appreciable effect. Sir Robert Giffen believes that the period of extraordinary demands is now completed, and that, with the further additions to the supplies which seem to be probable, a rise in gold prices may occur.

But it must not be forgotten that the effects of these extraordinary demands are, to some extent, cumulative. By the very influence, which they exert on the value of gold, they encourage repetition. They raise that value, and, in the absence of the controlling influence

---

[1] Qq. 18,173, etc.

[2] He was unwilling to compute definitely the Austro-Hungarian demand, which he himself did not regard as "ever likely to be so serious" as that of Germany or the United States. Lower estimates have been made by other authorities (*e.g.*, Prof. E. Nassé).

of a bimetallic system, cause a greater divergence from silver; and the tendency of gold to rise, and of silver to fall, disposes those who hoard, whether they be individuals, as in India, or governments in their war-chests, as in Europe (for the position of Russia is apparently not singular in this respect[1]) to accumulate gold rather than silver. The recent attempt—whether or not it be pronounced or proved abortive—to introduce a gold standard into India may also be traced directly to the divergence between the metals.[2] In this way the suspension of the free coinage of silver, both at a previous stage in recent monetary history by the closing of the mints of the Latin Union, and now by the action of the Indian Government, has tended to increase the demand for gold.

It may be true—and statistical evidence points, as Sir Robert Giffen has shown,[3] in this direction, that, owing partly to the silver-purchase Acts in the United States, and partly to the demands for token and subsidiary coinages, and for importation into India, the total consumption of silver has been larger since the suspension of free coinage in 1873 than before that date; and the fact that silver prices had not altered would furnish corroborative evidence. But it may still be argued that, if the bimetallic system had been in operation, the experience of the past points to the probability that the place now occupied by gold in the currencies of the world would have been taken to some extent by silver,

---

[1] *Cf.* Dunbar: "Theory and History of Banking," p. 129, on the action of the Bank of France.

[2] *Cf.* Report of Indian Currency Committee, sec. 1.

[3] In evidence before Commission on Agriculture, q. 18,222.

and to that extent the drain on the supplies of gold would have been relieved.[1]

For demands, which are extraordinary, may abate, and yet leave an influence behind. Under ordinary conditions,[2] with the progress of population, and the development of manufacture and trade, the demand for money tends to grow, if values are to preserve their nominal expression. Paper may indeed be used on an extended scale, but only to the degree that it is fiduciary, and does not rest on a metallic basis, does it relieve the demand for bullion. This point is sometimes overlooked, both by those who regard the paper as a substitute for the metal, and by those who consider that an accumulation in a bank of a stock of gold or silver is an idle hoard. In weighing, for example, the arguments of Tooke at the beginning of the century on the connection of the paper currency with the rise of prices, and of the resumption of cash payments with the fall, it must not be forgotten that he is only occupied with the question of the effects of the inconvertibility of the note, that is, of the absence of a metallic basis and the enlargement of the fiduciary issue. Again, it is sometimes urged that the purchases of silver in the United States under the Bland and Sherman Acts were useless accretions of idle metal; but, while those Acts may be condemned on other grounds, the accumulations were not idle, as they formed the basis of silver certificates,[3] and it is apparently admitted by competent inquirers that the rapid

---

[1] *Cf.* Prof. Foxwell in evidence before the same Commission, qq. 23,932, etc.

[2] *Cf.* Sir R. Giffen in paper in *Statistical Journal* for December, 1888, p. 762.

[3] *Cf.* Gibbs' "Colloquy on Currency,' pp. 71, 221.

growth of American business needs an expanding currency, and that there is no reason for holding that the actual effect at any rate of the Bland Act was to make the currency redundant.¹ In the case, once more, of some of the extraordinary demands for gold during the last twenty years, the hoarded metal seems to have been temporarily employed as a reserve against paper, and in some cases it has taken the place, not, it is true, of silver, but of inconvertible paper. Under these circumstances the extraordinary demand may itself pass away, but may leave behind an increase in the ordinary demand.

It is true that, with the development of credit, cheques and other substitutes for money—metallic or paper—are used to a wider extent; and that in the degree in which they permit of a greater economy of metal—in the degree, that is, in which a larger fabric of credit is raised on a narrower foundation of cash—they relieve the strain on the precious metals. It cannot be questioned that this development of credit has been advancing during the last twenty years; but there are reasons for thinking that some recent changes in the modes of conducting business may have increased rather than diminished the need for cash—that telegraphic transfers, for instance, may have taken the place of bills of exchange. It is certainly improbable that the growth of credit substitutes for money has kept pace with the new demands for gold.²

---

¹ *Cf.* Professor Taussig in 1892 on "The Silver Situation in the United States," with reference to the Bland Act; and also Sir R. Giffen in "Case against Bimetallism," viii., p. 180, and also Prof. Taussig's article in *Economic Journal* for December, 1893.

² *Cf.* Sir R. Giffen in evidence before Gold and Silver Commission, q. 556, also in "Essays in Finance," first series, p. 337, and in paper

For there is also a constant demand for fresh metal to replace the wear and tear of coins, and to meet the requirements of the arts. Dr. Soetbeer some ten years ago put the latter demand[1] at 13 millions, and at a later time, in 1889, Sir Robert Giffen stated[2] that about two-thirds of the annual production were taken for the arts, and that, if the consumption of India was included, the demand for "non-monetary" purposes was almost equal to the entire production. If these estimates are correct, the importance of the extraordinary demands of the last twenty years is rendered yet more manifest, and the sequel, left behind in the permanent addition to the ordinary demand, cannot but have exercised a serious influence on the value of the metal.

In view of this evidence, which, proceeding on different lines, and issuing from different quarters, yet converges to the same conclusion, it is impossible to doubt that the fall of prices shown by the index numbers is connected with monetary changes. The progress of improvement may have worked towards a fall, but by itself it is an insufficient explanation. If the principles of supply and demand be accurately conceived, and an increasing demand, coinciding with a diminishing supply, tends to cause an advance in value, then in the acknowledged recent extraordinary demands for gold, followed, as they inevitably must

in *Statistical Journal* for December, 1888, p. 763, Mr. Sauerbeck in evidence before Gold and Silver Commission, qq. 892, etc. *Cf.* contra evidence of Mr. Birch before the same Commission, qq. 1, 536, etc., and also that of Sir S. Montagu.

[1] "Materialien," iii., 3., 90,000 kilograms.

[2] "Case against Bimetallism," p. 85; Commission on Agriculture, q. 18,205.

be, and as they most assuredly have been, by an enlargement of the ordinary demands, we have a cause competent to produce the effect shown by the continuous fall of prices.

Nor do the criticisms passed on the validity of the evidence of the index numbers prejudice, but corroborate, this conclusion. Retail prices may not show so large a fall, where particulars can be obtained. But the admitted existence of greater friction in the retail trade accounts for the phenomenon, while it is very possible that in some particular cases an improvement in quality may have concealed a reduction in price. Wages, again, may have remained stationary, or fallen to a small extent; but, apart from the high probability of a real alteration in distribution favouring the wage-earner, we should expect the change to be more gradual. Such is the lesson of historical experience, and such is the inference to which *a priori* reasoning would conduct; for readjustments of wages can only be effected with friction and delay. This real rise of wages may also furnish part of the explanation of the comparative absence of the fall in retail prices, if that be true on a general view. They are the prices of goods into which manufacture has entered largely, and the difficulty of comparison of prices in their case may be partly ascribed to the possibility that it may have entered more largely at one time than another. The natural tendency of civilisation is to improve the methods, and reduce the cost, of the manufacturing process compared with that of obtaining the raw material; and, therefore, we should naturally look for a greater fall in manufactured goods. But, if there be a larger ingredient of labour in their manufacture, and the distribution of wealth inclines in favour of the workman, his stationary, or increased, wages would tend to maintain the price, or even to raise it, compared with that of articles where the element of labour is less important. Nor, in any case, could we expect the change in prices to be uniform or universal, as it is modified by, as well as modifies, the environment in which it operates.

The more permanent effect on wages would probably be curtailed employment, though in a community, which was otherwise progressive, this might take the form, not of a positive diminution, but an increase relatively less than what would have occurred. For it is not likely that falling prices should stop production, but that they should retard its advance. If the employer sustains a real injury through an increase in the pressure of his obligations in consequence of an actual fall, and the uncertainty and depression engendered by the prospects of a further fall benumb his imagination, and he becomes less confident and alert, if business recovers from a period of shaken credit and pressure in the money market with less rapidity and completeness, if the burden of national and municipal indebtedness, so far as the interest is fixed, or admits only of tardy diminution, grows steadily heavier, these influences must tend *pro tanto* to diminish the volume of production, and, in spite of improvement in his relative economic position, the wage-earner must so far participate in the loss that, under other conditions, his improvement would have been greater.

Such is the evidence that we may expect to find in a modern community of the influence of falling prices due to comparative scarcity of metal; and we shall look in vain for any other. The operation of the cause, and its connection with its effects, cannot be detached from the surroundings, and submitted to isolated observation. It will inevitably be mingled with obscuring circumstance. We can rarely hope to meet with facts so obvious as to exclude a second interpretation; and we must rather be prepared to extort from unwilling facts the lessons they contain. All that we can reach is a high degree of probability; we shall be disappointed if we seek for unquestioned certainty. This limitation of the character of our conclusions, as we saw in the opening chapter, is incident to the moral and political sciences, because we are debarred from instituting decisive experiments under rigid conditions. We are compelled to observe the course of events, and to watch experiments conducted, not with a view to the pure attainment of scientific truth, but with the object of advancing the public utility, or avoiding an injury, immediate or threatened, to the public welfare. But, if we do not discover certainty, we ought not on that account to set aside the evidence of high probability as inadequate to the establishment of speculative conclusions sufficient for guidance in practical policy. To acquiesce in an attitude of such despondent indolence is to condemn speculation to sterility, and practice to inaction.

We may now inquire whether in the case before us there is this evidence of high probability. It is difficult, if not impossible, to return a negative answer. On the one side there is evidence of a fall in wholesale prices, and on the other of a series of extraordinary demands for gold, which must have tended to increase its value for the time, and to leave behind a permanent addition to the ordinary demands. And these extraordinary demands, and this consequent tendency to an increase in the ordinary demands, have occurred with a production, which until the last few years was steadily declining from the level reached at the Californian and Australian discoveries. Here, then, we have a cause competent to produce the effect, and we have the effect produced. Such is the chief piece of evidence; and it is corroborated in various ways.

In a progressive community we should expect the volume of production to increase; and, in an address to the Economic Section of the British Association in 1887, Sir Robert Giffen, taking[1] the production of coal and of pig-iron, the receipts from railway goods traffic, the clearances of shipping in foreign trade, and the consumption of tea and sugar, showed that a decline had undoubtedly occurred in the ratio of increase in the period from 1875 to 1885 as compared with the two previous decennia. He was disinclined to attribute this decrease to foreign competition, partly because, as he urged, it was not in the foreign trade that any "check worth mentioning" had occurred; and for similar reasons he dismissed as inadequate the reduction of the hours of labour, the unfavourable seasons in agriculture, and the partial loss of our natural advantages in coal and iron. He observed, indeed—and to this point we shall return—that the growth of population, the diminution in pauperism, and the increase of the deposits in the savings banks, and of the assessments of houses, conflicted with the supposition of a real and permanent check, and that, as

[1] *Cf.* Report of British Association for 1887, pp. 806, etc.

the staple industries declined, the miscellaneous occupations grew, and therefore statistics of diminution based on these staple industries might be consistent with a change, not in the rate, but in the direction, of the total increase. In spite of these considerations he arrived at the general conclusion that some check had been offered to the rate of material growth, that the check, even if "too small to be measured by general statistics," was sufficient to produce no little "amount of *malaise*," and that the *malaise* was "largely accounted for" by the fall of prices. Sir Robert Giffen himself was then inclined to attribute little real importance to this fall; but the degree of importance, which different observers attach, must depend on the amount of influence, which they think that this feeling of *malaise* is likely to exert, and on the rate of material progress which, in the absence of such counteraction, might have been expected in a progressive community.

Nor are the facts of the decline of pauperism, the growth of population, and the increase of the deposits in the savings banks, and of house assessments, in conflict with what might have been expected. According to the last census, indeed,[1] the rate of increase of population has declined; but this fact, which is common to other communities, may be due to a rise in the standard of comfort. This very rise, however, is but one illustration of the change apparently proceeding in the distribution of wealth. In a progres-

---

[1] Vol. iv., General Report, ii., 1. "Not only" was the "increase absolutely less than in the previous decennium, 1871-81, but the rate of increase was lower than in any previous decennial period in the century."

sive community, where a real change of this nature is being effected, we should expect to see a decline of pauperism, a growth in the deposits in savings banks, and an increase in the assessments of houses. In most of the countries, where industry is organised on modern lines, and the manufacturing and commercial development of the age has been fully initiated, statistical evidence supports the conception of a real change in distribution—of a tendency, as M. Leroy Beaulieu has put it,[1] to a diminished inequality of conditions. And this tendency, which may be said to be placed beyond the reach of serious dispute, would lead, in the absence of some counteracting cause, to an increase of wages. That wages had been stationary might, therefore, seem to tell in favour of a fall of prices, due to some monetary cause, rather than against it, and to be consistent with the view that the position of the wage-earner would have been better without the fall. Again, the statistical evidence, as Sir Robert Giffen states[2] it before the Commission on Agriculture, shows that between 1870 and 1880 there was a rise of wages, and that between 1880 and 1893 in a few cases there had been a fall, but that in the great majority wages had remained stationary. It is, as we have seen, in accord with the probable operation of the cause for the effects to be manifest in wages only after some delay.

Passing from wages to profits, Sir Robert Giffen,

---

[1] In his "Essai sur la Répartition des Richesses."
[2] Q. 18,105, and appendix, table vi. (vol. ii.); *cf.* for more details paper in *Statistical Journal* for Dec., 1888; *cf.* also paper by Mr. A. L. Bowley in *Statistical Journal* for June, 1895, vol. viii., pt. ii.

in evidence given before the same Commission on Agriculture, states[1] that, down to about 1875-9, the assessment of profits for income tax, taking the nominal values per head, had increased; that after 1875-9 it had remained stationary, and that about 1890-93 it again exhibited a slight increase. This evidence points to the conclusion of a relative decline in profits from 1875-9 to 1890, as before 1875-9 the assessment was growing faster than the population, whereas in the subsequent period it was only growing as fast.

Hitherto the matter has been considered from what may be distinguished as the negative side. We have been asking whether there is reason for supposing that, if the cause had been absent, the effects might have been different. If we now turn to the positive side we find it difficult to dispute the general trend of the evidence. Within the last twenty years four Royal Commissions have been engaged on the question of depression. The Gold and Silver Commission was appointed *co nomine* to investigate the divergence between the values of the metals. It was appointed because the previous Commission on Trade Depression had, in the course of its inquiries, suspected the operation of some deep-seated cause connected with the metals.[2] Besides the Depression of Trade Commission, two Commissions have inquired into depression in Agriculture, one under the Chairmanship of the Duke of Richmond, and the other, which is now sitting, under that of Mr. Shaw Lefevre. The very fact of the appointment of these Commissions

---

[1] Q. 18,101, and appendix, table iv.
[2] *Cf.* Final Report, sec. 722, and Third Report.

may be taken as evidence of the reality of that *malaise*, which Sir Robert Giffen described as the natural consequence of falling prices. The feeling of depression and uncertainty, and the opinion that there was no agreed and obvious cause, may be taken as testimony—*quantum valeat*—to the likelihood of some underlying cause, such as a change in the relation of gold to commodities. Nor is there any serious question of the fact that the decline of profits formed the burden of the complaint before the Depression of Trade Commission; and that the two Commissions on Agriculture have repeated the same tale —and in the case of the latter in more urgent and emphatic language—of the fall of rents and the disappearance of farming profits.

This is as we should expect. That falling prices should especially affect the margin of profits, and that they should exercise a yet more destructive influence on that "margin of a margin," which, as Sir Robert Giffen has expressively put it, represents the rent of the landlord, accords with *a priori* speculation. It is true that other causes may also have been operating both in trade and agriculture. The period following the Franco-German war was one of extraordinary business activity, and, it may be added, of unhealthy excitement, and some reaction was inevitable. But the peculiar feature of the last twenty years has been that the depression, unlike its predecessors, has seemed perpetual. Probably in part at least for this reason some observers have even urged that the effects of the notorious Baring crisis, by being extended over a longer period, have proved more injurious than might have been the case, had the original crash not been averted. It is because they looked for a recovery which did not come.

In agriculture also it is true that at the time of the Duke of Richmond's Commission the influence of bad seasons counted for something, and the growth of foreign competition has since counted for more. But the opinion is widely entertained that, in view of the depression in other countries, some more general cause must also be in operation; and on *a priori* grounds it is not unlikely that the *malaise* should be more pronounced in agriculture than in other industries. It is an industry on which the burden of fixed charges, which can only be altered at long intervals, bears with especial weight. The obligations of an employer are current for shorter periods, and, while a continuous fall of prices may be repeatedly producing fresh disturbances, and destroy the narrow margin of profit, yet he is constantly entering into new obligations and ridding himself of the old. The burdens upon agriculture do not admit of such frequent adjustment. Rents may be lowered, but mortgages may bear an interest, which cannot be changed without delay, and yet has to be met from the diminished rental. The disturbance also of exchange between silver-using and gold-using countries necessitates, as we have seen, some readjustment, which must be accomplished by an alteration in the silver or the gold prices of the articles, which form the subject of commercial intercourse. One of the competitors of the English farmer has been the Indian cultivator; and it is agreed that until recently no change was manifest in silver prices in India. There must, therefore, have occurred—as undoubtedly there has occurred, to whatever cause it be ascribed—an alteration in the gold price of wheat in England. The *vis inertiæ* resisting change has proved greater in the sluggish conservative East than in the quick movement and active bustle of the Western World; and, without discussing further a controverted question, it seems to be impossible that this change has not *pro tanto* imposed some disadvantage on the English farmer.[1] Of the general hindrances to the development of trade with India, presented by the difficulties of exchange, especially in the case of the Lancashire cotton industry, no more need be said than that it is unquestionable that they have exercised some prejudicial influence, and that, while in their initiation they may be primarily due to the suspension of the free coinage of silver, in their aggravation they are connected with the rise in the value of gold.

Nor, finally, must we be misled by the expression, a "scarcity" of gold; and lightly acquiesce in the assurance[2] that no such scarcity is evident. The testimony adduced in support of such a contention admits of a different interpretation from that given by those who advance it. The accumulation of gold in bank reserves may be due to a desire to hoard the more valuable metal, or, for a time at least, to stagnating trade; and the rate of discount seems to be properly regarded as an index of the movement to and fro of gold, of its passage into and out of the country, into and out of the channels of trade. Matters will, and must, adjust themselves to the altered level of

[1] *Cf.* Prof. Foxwell in evidence before Commission on Agriculture, q. 23,686. The present influence of inconvertible paper on the supply and price of wheat from Argentina is similar.

[2] *Cf.* Lord Farrer before the same Commission, qq. 38,969, etc.

prices, and, on a strict scientific view, a scarcity of gold means no more than that it is relatively less abundant than before. The fact that prices have sunk is evidence that the relation between gold and commodities has altered—that the gold has become less and the commodities more abundant.

In the light of these converging lines of evidence it seems impossible to doubt the existence of a causal connection between the recent fall of prices and the monetary changes of the last twenty years. The degree of probability is so high as to amount to practical certainty; and in such inquiries we cannot hope to pass beyond this point. We must rest content with evidence such as this, or we must dismiss such investigations as altogether futile and impossible.

Of the prospects of the future it does not fall within the scope of the present inquiry to treat. The past few years have witnessed a notable increase in the supplies of gold from the mines, and, setting aside the possible requirements of India, a cessation of the extraordinary demands. But those extraordinary demands have left behind an increase in the ordinary demands; and the monetary position is so uncertain that it is impossible to say that some fresh extraordinary demand may not arise. The consumption in the arts is estimated to be a very large proportion of the present supplies.[1] The natural growth of population

---

[1] In his report for 1894 the Director of the United States Mint computed that, taking into consideration the consumption in the arts and the export to India, there was in 1893 about as much gold available for coinage purposes as there was of both metals in the years 1866-73. But for succeeding years he anticipated a considerable increase (*Cf.* vol. iii., appendix xii. of evidence before Commission on Agriculture).

and of production constitutes, so far as credit instruments are not employed, and to some extent even when these are used, a continuous increase in the ordinary demand. Some backward nations, like India, pass on their way to the development of credit through a period of adaeration, as it is termed, when they adopt cash payments in lieu of barter, and require more and not less metal than before. Nor were the effects of the Californian and Australian discoveries, which had not been paralleled for abundance since the mineral wealth of Mexico and Peru was poured into the world, by any means as great as had been confidently thought. So soon indeed were they apparently completed, that it seems premature to look for any very considerable rise of prices from the fresh supplies of Southern Africa and Western Australia.[1] Metallic mining is proverbially a lottery, though it is true that in the course of history, silver, and latterly also gold, have become more fully subject to ordinary commercial influences, and lend themselves more readily to safe prediction. But the liability of prophecy to err is not less common than the temptation to predict; and the past history of the precious metals supplies abundant evidence of the pertinence of such considerations. The present inquiry is complete when we have traced to our own days the tale of the more notable changes in general prices, which the modern world has already witnessed; and we may contentedly allow the prophet undisputed sway over the uncertain region of the future.

[1] The application, however, of the cyanide process has also led to an increased production from the older sources of supply.

THE END.

www.ingramcontent.com/pod-product-compliance
Lightning Source LLC
Chambersburg PA
CBHW020909230426
43666CB00008B/1379